# the GIN DRINKER'S YEAR

**Drinking** and **Other Things** to do with **Gin; Day** by **Day, Season** by **Season**

Tara Richardson

An Hachette UK Company
www.hachette.co.uk

First published in Great Britain in 2021 by Pyramid,
an imprint of Octopus Publishing Group Ltd
Carmelite House
50 Victoria Embankment
London, EC4Y 0DZ
www.octopusbooks.co.uk

Distributed in the US by
Hachette Book Group
1290 Avenue of the Americas
4th and 5th Floors
New York, NY 10104

Distributed in Canada by
Canadian Manda Group
664 Annette St.
Toronto, Ontario, Canada M6S 2C8



ISBN: 978-0-7537-3455-1

A CIP catalogue record for this book is available from the British Library

Printed and bound in China

10 9 8 7 6 5 4 3 2 1

Publisher: Lucy Pessell
Designer: Hannah Coughlin
Junior Editor: Sarah Kennedy
Editorial Assistant: Emily Martin
Recipe Development: Matthew Robertson, Jane Birch
Production Controller: Serena Savini
Picture acknowledgements: Sicha/rawpixel.com

# CONTENTS

# INTRODUCTION

Welcome to the best and booziest of years. Happily, this is your guide to many more great and ginny years, as we've left the moveable feasts such as Easter free to do their own thing and not tied them to a specific date, meaning you can use this book year after year. So, Easter need never interfere with your National Liquorice Day celebrations or spoil the fun that is Count de Negroni's birthday. But don't worry, you can still make Gin and Pistachio Truffles as a sweet Easter treat.

We are as fond of a silly segue and a nonsense reason to mix ourselves a snifter as we are of gin, but it's okay if you aren't – this book will still do whatever you need it to do if you skip to the index of recipes at the back of the book.

Let's be-gin.

For those of you not well-practised in the art of cocktail making or well-versed in its lingo, here are some tips, hacks and techniques to help you. Honestly, it's not that hard and you don't need loads of fancy kit, although a cocktail shaker is more-or-less THE MOST NECESSARY OF ALL BITS OF KIT EVER. Yes, we all know someone who's attempted to do it with two pint glasses, but do any of us know anyone who that worked out well for? No. No we don't.

## Shaking

We shake a cocktail for four reasons: to mix it, to chill it, to dilute it and to create texture through aeration. There are two types of shaker: the three-part shaker (or Cobbler shaker) and the two-part shaker (or Boston shaker). The Boston shaker is probably the one you'll recognize and is by far the cheapest and easiest to come by.

*If Using a Three-Part Shaker:*
You know your stuff so read no further.

*If Using A Two-Part Shaker:*
Unless the method tells you otherwise: add the ingredients to the glass or smaller part of your shaker, and then two-thirds fill the larger part with ice. Bring the two parts together, clasp firmly with both hands and shake vigorously for 5–10 seconds.

*Dry Shaking:*
We whip or 'dry-shake' a cocktail without ice to incorporate egg whites into the drink, and to create a luxuriously fluffy texture and mouth feel, usually in a sour or a fizz. This binds the mixture together, so once we have dry shaken, we then need to shake again but this time with ice, as you would with any other shaken drink.

## Straining

After shaking or stirring, we need to strain the drink so that the chipped ice and anything else left in the shaker, like herbs or fruit, do not end up in the drink.
If you are using a three-part shaker, you will have a strainer built in, but with a two-part shaker you will need a cocktail strainer, which is clasped over the top before pouring the drink into the glass.

*Double Straining:*
For any drink served 'up' or without ice, like a Daiquiri, strain additionally through a small sieve or tea strainer to ensure that absolutely nothing that was in the shaker or mixing glass ends up in the drink. We always want to taste the ingredients, but sometimes we don't want to see them.

## Blending

Blending allows us to incorporate ice into a drink, creating a smooth Frappé-like texture. You can do this in a domestic blender or food processor.

## Ice

Strange as it may seem, ice is the most important component of any mixed drink. (Well, we think it's the second most important ingredient after gin, but let's not quibble.) Ice is your best friend, so please make sure you have plenty of it. It chills liquid to the desired temperature, it dilutes and it softens the rougher edges of strong spirits. Ice is just as important in the making and serving of a cocktail as any other ingredient listed in the recipe, so good-quality ice must be a mainstay of any home bar. Shop-bought ice cubes are great, but if you can, build up a stash in your freezer so that you have ice cubes ready to hand. Don't use any cubes that have cracked – they can mess with your dilution, and make your beautiful concoctions a little less beautiful on the eye. On the occasions where a recipe calls for crushed ice, if you have a fancy ice-crushing contraption, lovely, but wrapping cubed ice in a tea towel and bashing the daylights out of it with a rolling pin or unwanted ornament will give you exactly the same result.

## Gin

Happily, there are more brands of gins out there than even the most enthusiastic of us will ever get around to trying, but when infusing gin, or making cocktails for the first time, we recommend choosing a classic dry gin rather than anything too flavoured. By all means experiment once you've tried something a couple of times, but the recipes in this book work on the assumption that your gin is straight-up gin and not already infused with the flavours of every tree and spice of every continent.

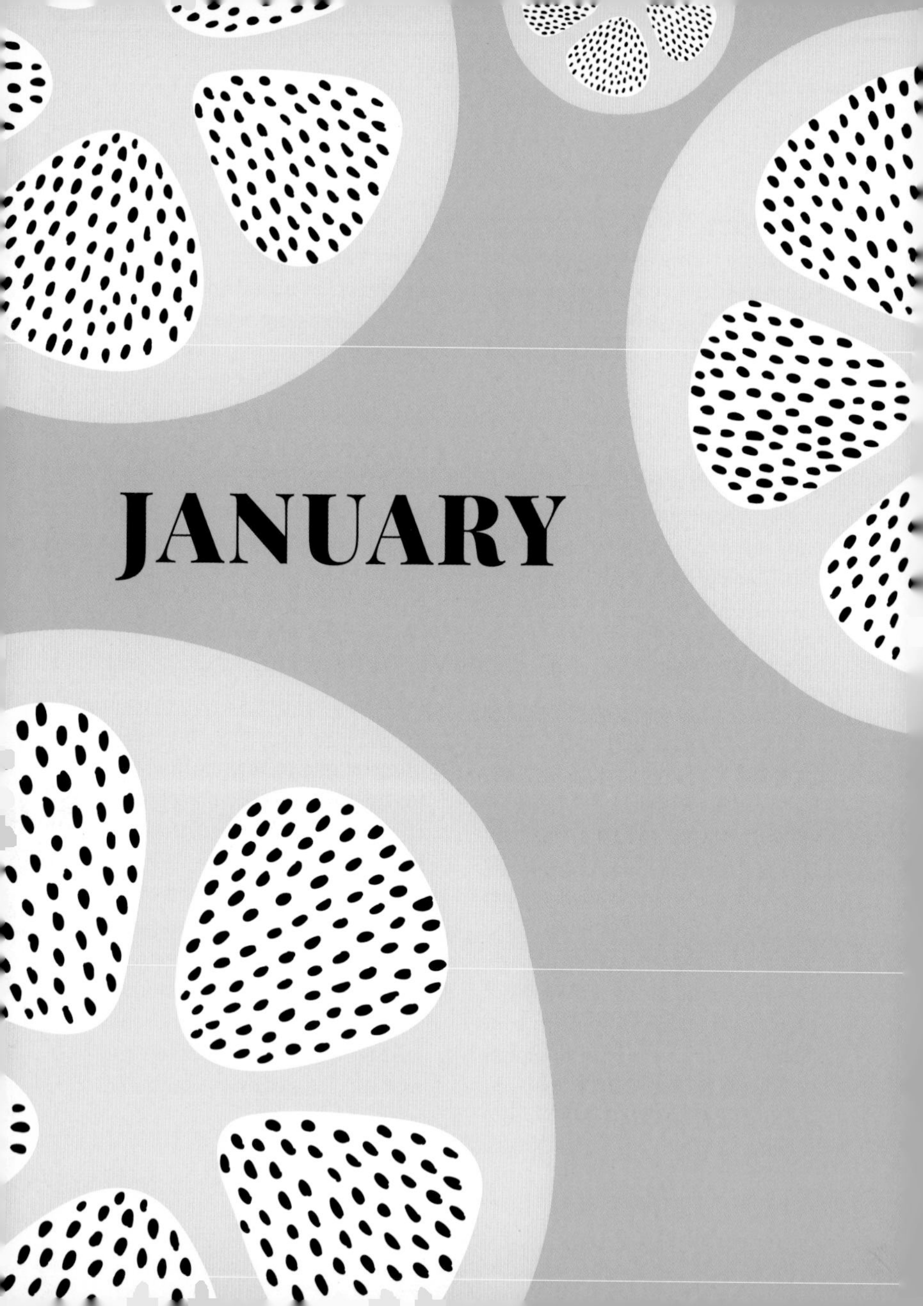
JANUARY

## 1 JANUARY

### New Year's Day

If you're nursing a hangover after your New Year's celebrations, try a Red Snapper for your 'hair of the dog' cure.

Before the vodka-based Bloody Mary became popular with the sore-of-head in the 1920s, a gin and tomato juice was the morning-after treatment of choice.

### Red Snapper

*2 measures gin*
*5 measures tomato juice*
*½ measure lemon juice*
*4 dashes Worcestershire sauce*
*2 dashes Tabasco sauce*
*1 tbsp horseradish cream*
*pinch of salt*
*pinch of cracked black pepper*
*celery, lemon and green olive, to garnish*

Add all of the ingredients to a highball glass, stirring in cubed ice as you go. Garnish with a celery stick, lemon wedge and green olive.

## 2 JANUARY

1 January is always a bit of a false start, but now you're probably ready to join in with Dry January. Kick things off as you mean to go on with a nice, crisp, dry gin.

## 3 JANUARY

The 'Pink Gin' on today's shop shelves is a sugary, fruity affair and a hundred thousand miles across the sea from the original. Vastly popular in its day, Pink Gin was conceived in Plymouth in the 1800s by naval officers. It was a means of making a tonic made from Angostura bitters, and prescribed for seasickness, more palatable. It worked.

The original Pink Gin is as bracing as a howling sou'westerly and really does shiver the timbers. But in the best of ways. →

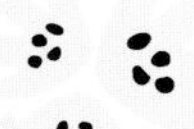

## Pink Gin

*2 measures gin*
*5 dashes Angostura bitters*
*still water, to top*

Add all of the ingredients to an old fashioned glass filled with cubed ice and stir briefly. No garnish.

## 4 January

*Gineral Knowledge: Bitters*
Cocktail bitters are blends of distilled grain alcohols which are then infused with natural ingredients including spices, herbs, roots, tree barks and fruit peels. They can be used as a kind of cocktail seasoning – adding a few drops will provide an intense flavour boost, rather like certain oils or vinegars in cooking. The most well-known and commonly used bitters are Angostura, Peychaud's and orange.

## 5 January
## Pink Gin Jellies

*Serves 4*

*100g (3½oz) caster sugar*
*4 leaves gelatine*
*100ml (3½fl oz) gin*
*150ml (¼ pint) Indian tonic water*
*50ml (2fl oz) ruby grapefruit or cranberry juice*
*raspberries, to decorate*

Put the sugar in a small saucepan with 250ml (8fl oz) water and heat, stirring until the sugar is dissolved.
Place 3 tablespoons of water in a heatproof bowl, add the gelatine and leave to soak for 5 minutes. Place the bowl over a saucepan of simmering water and heat gently until dissolved.
Remove from the heat and add the gin, tonic water, fruit juice and sugar syrup and stir well. Pour into glasses and chill for at least 3 hours or until set. Top with raspberries to decorate.

## 6 JANUARY

*Craft: Painted Bottles*
Once you've enjoyed all that lovely gin, you can turn the bottles into ornaments or table decorations with just a little paint. Clean the bottles and remove the labels. Once they're dry, paint them in your favourite colours, or even in a pattern. Acrylic paint is the best kind to use, as not all paints will adhere well to glass. If you're feeling extra fancy, why not finish them with a little gold leaf? These could make great table number holders for a wedding.

## 7 JANUARY

Mark the first 7 of the year with a toast to 007. We all know Bond likes his martini shaken not stirred, but he's also partial to a Vesper. In fact, this is the only truly acceptable occasion when a martini is shaken – and it's derived straight from the pages of Ian Fleming's first James Bond novel, *Casino Royale* (1953). A vigorous shake and the addition of Lillet Blanc dilutes and softens.

### Vesper Martini

*2½ measures gin*
*1 measure vodka*
*½ measure Lillet Blanc*
*lemon, to garnish*

Add all of the ingredients into the bottom of your cocktail shaker, and fill the top half of it with ice. Shake vigorously and double strain into a chilled martini glass. Garnish with a lemon twist.

## 8 JANUARY

Congratulations, you have finally finished the turkey. To celebrate, and welcome in a whole year of eating actual food, try this utterly delicious gin pasta. You heard...

### Gin Penne with Slow-Roasted Tomatoes

*Serves 4*

*150g (5oz) baby plum tomatoes, halved*
*olive oil, for drizzling*
*400g (13oz) penne pasta*
*50ml (2fl oz) gin*
*75ml (3fl oz) double cream*
*50g (2oz) grated Parmesan cheese*
*handful of chopped basil leaves*
*salt and black pepper*

Place the halved tomatoes in a roasting tin, drizzle over a little oil and season. Place in a preheated oven, 150°C (300°F), Gas Mark 2, for 20–25 minutes until lightly browned.

Meanwhile, cook the penne pasta according to the instructions on the packet.

Heat the gin in a small saucepan and simmer until reduced to about 1 tablespoon. Pour over the double cream and add the Parmesan, stirring.

Drain the pasta and return to its pan. Pour in the sauce and add the roasted tomatoes and basil leaves. Toss to mix well and serve immediately.

## 9 JANUARY

*Gineral Knowledge: Vermouth*

We have Italy to thank for more than penne alla gin (actually, probably just the penne). Italy gave us the drinkable version of vermouth; arguably the backbone of the martini.

Back in the early 17th century 'vermouth' was a medicinal fortified wine that contained the bitter-tasting herb, wormwood. ('Vermouth' being the French pronunciation of 'wermut' – the German word for 'wormwood').

But then, in the late 18th century, Italy started doing very clever things with it and introduced a sweet vermouth in 1786. Thank you, Italy.

## 10 JANUARY

'The proper union of gin and vermouth is a great and sudden glory; it is one of the happiest marriages on earth, and one of the shortest lived.'
*Bernard DeVoto*

## 11 JANUARY

*Gineral Knowledge: Beefeaters*
Among London's most iconic sights are the Yeoman Warders at the Tower of London, more commonly known as Beefeaters. They've been guarding the tower since Tudor times. Every year on their birthday, each Yeoman Warder is sent a bottle of gin from the Beefeater Distillery, the only Victorian gin-maker still operating in London.

## 12 JANUARY

### London Calling

*1½ measures gin*
*¾ measure lemon juice*
*¾ measure Fino sherry*
*½ measure sugar syrup*
*2 dashes Angostura bitters*
*lemon, to garnish*

Add all of the ingredients to your cocktail shaker, shake vigorously and strain into a chilled coupette glass. Garnish with a lemon twist.

## 13 JANUARY

### Celeriac Gin

January might seem like a dud month for fresh and seasonal ingredients to pair with your gin but it isn't. Behold ... the celeriac. Simply wash, peel and chop up a head of celeriac and put it in a container, cover it in 500ml (17fl oz) gin, put the lid on and let it infuse in a cool, dark place for 24 hours. Then strain it, keep it in an airtight container and you have a delicious base to a Bloody Mary that can be stored in the fridge for weeks.

## 14 JANUARY

Oops. Resolutions. Those things that other people make and stick to. It isn't too late. How about this: 'I resolve to try a different gin every month'?

## 15 JANUARY

On this day in 1994, Snoop Dogg released his seminal single *Gin & Juice*. The exact recipe for Gin & Juice is hazy but it's usually a mix of cranberry and orange and almost always calls for Tanqueray No. 10. Ooh wee!

## 16 JANUARY

If West Coast hip-hop doesn't do it for you then maybe this will. Fancy a sing-along?

*Ten green bottles, hanging on the wall, ten green bottles, hanging on the wall, and if one…*

What? You don't have ten green bottles? Well, there's only one way to solve that problem…

## 17 JANUARY

*Gineral Knowledge: Prohibition*

On this day in 1920, Prohibition began. In response to rising social difficulties stemming from the misuse of alcohol in the United States, The Volstead Act of 1920 was passed by Congress despite President Woodrow Wilson's veto. The Act prohibited the production, importation, transportation and sale of 'intoxicating liquors' – any substance that contained more than 0.5% alcohol.

In a sense it worked, as alcohol consumption dropped markedly, but it spawned an underground crime-wave largely driven by the illegal smuggling and production of alcohol. Oops.

# 18 January

Coincidentally, yesterday was also Al Capone's birthday. Born in 1899, 'Scarface' attained notoriety as the kingpin of an organized crime empire which was built on the profits of bootlegging and other Prohibition crimes. His gang smuggled vast quantities of gin into Chicago's South side. Unlike the mellow gin imported by the North Side Mob, Capone's gin was poorly made 'bathtub gin', and flavourings and sweeteners were required to mask its rough edges. Capone became partial to a Southside – a fresh, lively and limey cocktail that could mask all the evils of the world.

## Southside

*2 measures gin*
*¾ measure lime juice*
*¾ measure sugar syrup*
*6 mint leaves*
*mint, to garnish*

Add all of the ingredients to your cocktail shaker, shake vigorously and double strain into a chilled coupette glass. Garnish with a mint leaf.

# 19 January

A refreshing cucumber twist on the classic Southside.

## East Side

*2 measures gin*
*1 measure lime juice*
*¾ measure sugar syrup*
*3 cubes cucumber*
*6 mint leaves*
*cucumber, to garnish*

Muddle the cucumber and mint in the bottom of a cocktail shaker. Add the remaining ingredients, shake, and then double strain into a chilled coupette glass. Garnish with a slice of cucumber.

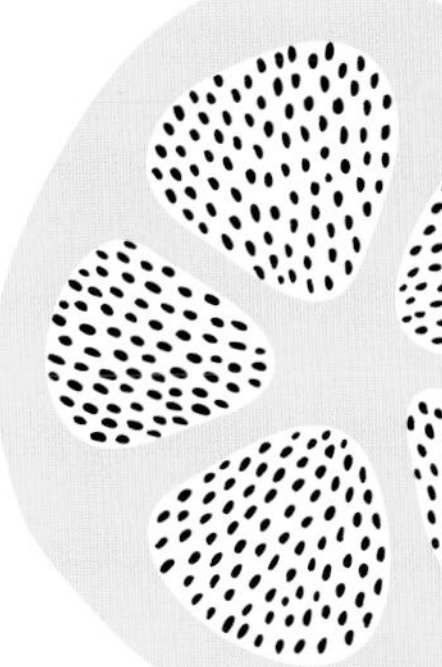

## 20 JANUARY

A classic from the *Savoy Cocktail Book* (1930), and a yet another riff on the Southside. Make sure you use freshly squeezed orange juice.

### Paradise

*1¾ measures gin*
*½ measure apricot brandy*
*1½ measures orange juice*
*2 dashes orange bitters*
*orange, to garnish*

Add all of the ingredients to your cocktail shaker, shake vigorously and strain into a coupette glass. Garnish with an orange twist.

## 21 JANUARY

*Gineral Knowledge: London Dry Gin*

Contrary to popular belief, you do not need to be in London to make London Dry Gin. The term refers to the style and production methods pioneered by London gin-makers in the years after the invention of 'continuous distillation'. This process – invented by an Irishman named Aenus Coffey in the early 1800s – yielded a more consistent and, indeed, drier final product. There are still very strict rules governing its production, and to be called 'London Dry Gin', the ingredients must be of completely natural origin, the dominant botanical must be juniper and no ingredients may be added after distillation other than water and the tiniest bit of sugar. Additionally, the finished product must be at least 37.5% ABV.

## 22 JANUARY

*Famous Birthday: Lord Byron*

On this day in 1788, poet, politician and all-round bad boy Lord Byron was born. Famously described as 'mad, bad and dangerous to know', Byron was one of the most popular writers of his time – and is once said to have announced: 'gin-and-water is the source of all my inspiration'.

## 23 JANUARY

The Doobs Martini is an excellent martini alternative, with powerful notes of sour hedgerow fruit that cut through the seemingly endless January nights.

### Doobs Martini

*1¾ measures gin*
*1 measure sloe gin*
*¾ measure dry vermouth*
*4 dashes orange bitters*
*orange, to garnish*

Add all of the ingredients to a cocktail shaker or mixing glass, and fill with cubed ice. Stir for 30 seconds, and strain into a chilled martini glass. Garnish with an orange rind twist.

## 24 JANUARY

*Gineral Knowledge: Gin*
Gin as we know it today is a grain spirit flavoured with botanicals – most notably juniper – which originated in Holland in the 1500s and was and known then as 'genever'.

Gin production in England began around the start of the 1700s, but the resulting liquid was usually crude, haphazard and down-right dangerous.

## 25 JANUARY
## Burns Night

Today it's traditional to celebrate the life and works of Scottish poet Robert Burns. Try a Rabbie's Martinez – a ginny riff on the classic Bobby Burn's cocktail.

### Rabbie's Martinez

*2 measures gin*
*1 measure sweet vermouth*
*¼ measure Bénédictine*
*2 dashes Angostura bitters*
*lemon, to garnish*

Add all of the ingredients to a cocktail shaker or mixing glass, and fill with cubed ice. Stir for 30 seconds, and strain into a chilled coupette glass. Garnish with a lemon twist.

## 26 JANUARY

*Gineral Knowledge: Sour*

Sours were first described by Jerry Thomas in his book *How to Mix Drinks* (1862). Derived from the basic principles of punch making, sours are the building blocks of cocktail creation.

A sour is the epitome of balance in a cocktail; you need a boozy ingredient, a sweet ingredient, and an acidic ingredient; the result of which will, if made properly, be a cocktail that is greater than the sum of its parts. There are whisky sours and gin sours but sours can also come in disguise. Is a daiquiri a sour? Yep. Is a margarita a sour? Sure. Is a Tom Collins a gin sour topped up with soda water? Kind of, yes. Always simple on paper, but so very easy to mess up, sours are the ultimate test of precision, technique and specificity in drinks-making.

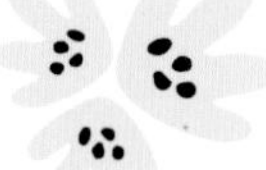

## 27 JANUARY

The very simplest of sours, and really the building block of all drinks making, the Fix was first recorded in Jerry Thomas's *How to Mix Drinks*.

### Fix

*2 measures gin*
*1 measure lemon juice*
*¾ measures sugar syrup*
*seasonal fruit, to garnish*

Add all of the ingredients to a rocks glass filled with crushed ice. Churn, and garnish with seasonal fruit of your choosing.

## 28 JANUARY

On this day in 1813, Jane Austen's *Pride & Prejudice* was published. And we'd like to think that it is a universally acknowledged truth that every literary milestone should be marked with a toast to the writer.

## 29 JANUARY

*Gineral Knowledge: Exports*
The UK is the largest exporter of gin in the world, with exports worth more than £600 million in 2018. Don't worry if you're in the UK, though – there's still plenty left! Brits bought 73 million bottles of the wonderful stuff in the same year.

## 30 JANUARY

*Famous Birthday: Franklin Delano Roosevelt*
FDR served as the 32nd president of the United States from 1933 until his death in 1945. Today marks his birthday and the day can't slide without a toast as, without him, we might not (almost definitely wouldn't) have discovered this version of the Dirty Martini. Also known as the FDR Martini, the key ingredient here is olive brine. The dry saltiness of the Dirty Martini is loathed and loved in equal measure depending on the drinker's feelings about olives. Delicious. Or awful. →

### Dirty Martini

*2½ measures gin*
*¼ measure dry vermouth*
*½ measure olive brine*
*olives, to garnish*

Add all of the ingredients to a cocktail shaker or mixing glass, and fill with cubed ice. Stir for 30 seconds, and strain into a chilled martini glass. Garnish with olives.

## 31 JANUARY

January has come to an end. Celebrate with a G&T.

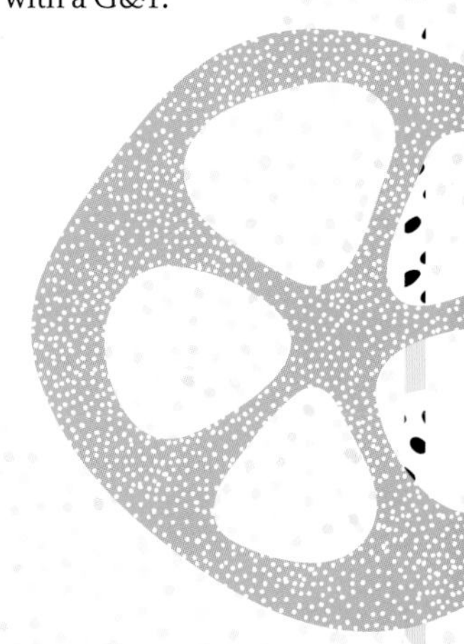

# FEBRUARY

# 1 FEBRUARY

*Famous Birthday: Clark Gable*
Clark Gable was born on 1 February 1901. In the 1958 film *Teacher's Pet*, in which Gable starred alongside Doris Day, his character makes a martini using a method apparently favoured by the actor himself: he pours gin into a glass, then gently shakes the bottle of vermouth, just enough to wet the cork. Then he wipes the vermouth cork around the edge of the glass, before drinking with ice. Why not give it a try?

# 2 FEBRUARY

## National Grapefruit Month (US)

The grapefruit is a hybrid citrus fruit – a cross between a pomelo and a sweet orange. Packed with vitamin C, vitamin B6, potassium, thiamin, niacin, and antioxidants, it's a true breakfast superfood. For a super, decadent breakfast snifter, try a Fair Lady.

### Fair Lady

*1½ measures gin*
*2 dashes Cointreau*
*2 measures grapefruit juice*
*1 measure egg white*
*caster sugar*

Dip the rim of a chilled coupette glass firstly in the egg white, then in the caster sugar to create a sugar frosting. Add the rest of the ingredients, including the remaining egg white, into your cocktail shaker, shake vigorously and double strain. No garnish.

## 3 February

*Gineral Knowledge: 'Cocktail'*
The earliest mention of the word 'cocktail' in reference to a drink was on 20 March 1798 in the *London Morning Post and Gazetteer* (how's that for historical?) In the newspaper's satirical account, it was consumed by Pitt the Younger at the Axe and Gate Tavern at the corner of Downing Street and Whitehall, which was later torn down to expand the Prime Minister's residence.

## 4 February

*Gineral Knowledge: The Gin Craze*
The Gin Craze was a time in the first half of the 1700s when British consumption of gin rose so rapidly that it became a public health concern. The government passed a series of legislation, known as the Gin Acts, to try to control the production and consumption of gin.

## 5 February

On this day in 1968, the song *Jennifer Juniper* by Scottish singer-songwriter Donovan was released.

## 6 February

As the celebration of grapefruit is intended to be a month-long affair, try this aromatic and ever-so-slightly fruity gin spritz with a grapefruit garnish.

### P&T

*1½ measures pink gin*
*½ measure strawberry liqueur*
*½ measure lemon juice*
*equal parts tonic and soda water, to top*
*rosemary and grapefruit, to garnish*

Build all the ingredients in a large wine glass full of cubed ice, stir briefly and garnish with a sprig of rosemary and a slice of grapefruit.

## 7 FEBRUARY

*Famous Birthday: Charles Dickens*
Charles Dickens was born on 7 February 1812. Gin-loving fans of his work will be spoilt for choice for references to our favourite tipple. In *The Pickwick Papers*, Sam Weller, who confesses he is feeling a little 'staggery this morning', concocts a rather fine hangover remedy by mixing together a bracing cocktail of 'British Hollands [gin] and the fragrant essence of the clove'.
Sam certainly has a better time of it than the unfortunate rag-and-bone man Krook (another of Dickens's gin-drinking characters) who falls victim to spontaneous combustion in *Bleak House*.

## 8 FEBRUARY

*Game: Ten-Gin Bowling*
If you've ended up with a few empty gin bottles after the festive season, we suggest washing them out and using them to play ten-gin bowling, with the gin bottles replacing the skittles.

## 9 FEBRUARY

*Know Your Glassware: Balloon Glass*
The balloon glass – also known as a copa de balon – is a long-stemmed, globe-shaped glass that looks beautiful and is perfect for gin and tonics. It's a must if you like your G&T ice-cold, as the bowl of the glass allows plenty of space for ice, while the stem means the warmth of your hands won't melt it, diluting your drink.

## 10 February

In New Orleans, celebrations for Mardi Gras – also known as 'Fat Tuesday' – would usually be well under way by now. A riot of colour, the parades draw crowds of thousands each year. If all of that sounds a bit exhausting, sit back and quietly contemplate things with a New Orleans Dry Martini – bone-dry and with a welcome snap of anise coming from the absinthe.

### New Orleans Dry Martini

*2½ measures gin*
*½ measure dry vermouth*
*2 drops absinthe (or Pernod)*
*lemon, to garnish*

Add all of the ingredients to a cocktail shaker or mixing glass filled with cubed ice. Stir for 30 seconds and strain into a chilled martini glass. Garnish with a twist of lemon.

## 11 February

Valentine's Day is nearly upon us. Make of that what you will, but whatever your thoughts are on a day seemingly designed to make us feel anxious about being single or robbed for being not, make time for a Hanky Panky. Not 'some' hanky panky (although we won't stop you if you do) – 'a' Hanky Panky: a subtle twist on the Martinez cocktail, created by Ada Coleman at the Savoy Hotel in the early 1900s.

### Hanky Panky

*2 measures gin*
*1 measure sweet vermouth*
*1 tbsp Fernet Branca*
*orange, to garnish*

Add all of the ingredients to a cocktail shaker or mixing glass, and fill with cubed ice. Stir for 30 seconds, and strain into a chilled martini glass. Garnish with an orange twist

## 12 FEBRUARY

*Gineral Knowledge: Ada Coleman*
Ada 'Coley' Coleman (1875–1966), was head bartender (the only woman to fill the role) at the American Bar of the Savoy Hotel, where she worked for 23 years. Such was her popularity with customers, her retirement was announced in the national newspapers. Her most enduring recipe is that of the Hanky Panky, reportedly created for the actor Charles Hawtrey.

## 13 FEBRUARY

*Game: Spin the Bottle*
With just one day to go until Valentine's Day, why not play a quick round of spin the bottle? It's a good use of a gin bottle, and you might secure yourself a smooch for tomorrow as well.

## 14 FEBRUARY

## Valentine's Day

Celebrate or commiserate the day with a sharply flavoured raspberry martini, with a brisk ginny kick. Perfectly enjoyable on occasions other than Valentine's Day.

### Valentine Martini

*2 measures gin*
*¾ measure lime juice*
*¾ measure sugar syrup*
*6 raspberries*
*raspberry and lime, to garnish*

Add all of the ingredients to your cocktail shaker, shake vigorously, then double strain into a chilled martini glass and garnish with raspberries and a twist of lime.

## 15 FEBRUARY

*Gineral Knowledge: Gin*
Gin was first mentioned in the *Oxford English Dictionary* in 1714, and was defined as 'an infamous liquor'.

## 16 February

## National Almond Day (US)

Celebrate with an Army and Navy – a delicious gin sour, flavoured with almond. For those of you bothered about 'balance', this can be fiendishly difficult to get right, so ensure you measure your ingredients accurately and shake well. For those of you who don't mind at all, carry on as you were.

### Army & Navy

*2 measures gin*
*1 measure lemon juice*
*½ measure orgeat syrup*
*lemon, to garnish*

Add all of the ingredients to your cocktail shaker. Shake vigorously with cubed ice and double strain into a chilled coupette glass. Garnish with a lemon twist.

## 17 February

*Gineral Knowledge: Orgeat*

Orgeat is a syrup or cordial made by combining almonds, sugar and water. Rose water or orange flower may also be added to create a sweet and fragrant syrup that tastes not dissimilar to marzipan.

## 18 February

If National Almond Day hadn't got in the way, we might well have been celebrating Shrove Tuesday. Give your pancakes a sophisticated twist with a fruity sloe gin coulis.

### Pancakes with Blackcurrant & Sloe Gin Coulis

*Serves 4*

*100g (3½oz) plain flour*
*pinch of salt*
*2 eggs, beaten*
*300ml (½ pint) milk*
*2 tablespoons melted unsalted butter*
*knob of unsalted butter, for frying*

→

*For the coulis*
*50g (2oz) caster sugar*
*2 tablespoons sloe gin*
*125g (5oz) blackcurrants*

To make the coulis, place the caster sugar and the sloe gin in a pan. Slowly stir in the blackcurrants and heat gently until the sugar has dissolved. Simmer gently for 3–4 minutes until the fruit is soft. Pour into a food processor or blender and blend to a purée, then press through a sieve into a bowl to remove the pips. Set aside while you make the pancakes.
Sift the flour and salt into a large bowl and make a well in the centre. Pour the beaten eggs into the well, then gradually whisk into the flour mixture. Add the milk a little at a time, whisking to form a smooth batter. Stir in the melted butter.
Heat a little of the butter for frying in a 20cm (8in) frying pan. Add a ladleful of the batter and swirl around to coat the bottom of the pan. Cook for 1–2 minutes until golden, then flip over and cook for a further 1 minute. Remove from the pan and keep warm. →
Repeat with the remaining batter to make 8 pancakes, adding more butter if necessary.
To serve, fill each pancake with a little of the coulis.

## 19 FEBRUARY

A delicious twist on the gin sour, this is given savoury depth from the hedgerow fruit astringency of sloe gin.

### Sloe Gin Sour

*2 measures sloe gin*
*1 measure lemon juice*
*1 measure sugar syrup*
*½ measure egg white*
*2 dashes Peychaud's bitters*
*orange, to garnish*

Add all of the ingredients to your cocktail shaker and dry-shake without ice for 10 seconds, take the shaker apart and add cubed ice. Shake vigorously and double strain into an old fashioned glass filled with cubed ice. Garnish with an orange slice.

## 20 February

*Gineral Knowledge: Bathtub Gin*
The term 'bathtub gin' refers to the Prohibition-era practice, of enhancing un-flavoured grain alcohol (Moonshine) with the ingredients and flavours most closely associated with gin; things like juniper, citrus and spice. Basically, it was a way of making gin without needing a cumbersome and expensive thing like a distillery. The most common and practical vessel for achieving this was a domestic bathtub, which was big enough to yield the maker a decent return, whilst being small enough to conceal in the privacy of their own home.

## 21 February

Although we can be happy that we don't live in the times of bathtub gin, perhaps there is a way to update the concept for the 21st century. Run yourself a steaming hot bubble bath, and hop in – with a glass of your favourite gin cocktail, of course.

## 22 February

On this day in 2004, the last episode of *Sex and the City* aired. *SATC* immortalized the Cosmo cocktail and its popularity shows little sign of waning. Sadly, the absence of gin showed little sign of waning either, so we decided to do something about it and are very pleased to introduce you to The Cosmoginitan.

### The Cosmoginitan

*1½ measures gin*
*¾ measure Cointreau*
*½ measure lime juice*
*1½ measures cranberry juice*
*orange, to garnish*

Add all of the ingredients to your cocktail shaker. Shake vigorously with cubed ice and double strain into a chilled martini glass. Garnish with a flamed orange twist.

# 23 FEBRUARY

*Gineral Knowledge: Coriander/ Cilantro*

Coriander seed is the second most important botanical in gin production after juniper. Only the tiniest fraction of gins currently in production don't use coriander seed as a key ingredient, so be suspicious of any gin lover who claims they hate coriander. Coriander seed has earned the rather splendid nickname 'dizzy corn' thanks to its narcotic properties when consumed in very large quantities. Farmers around the world have noted that animals grazing around patches of coriander behave oddly afterwards. Others have noted that people consuming large quantities of gin behave oddly afterwards but we can deduce that these people are simply dizzy, and not odd.

# 24 FEBRUARY

## International I Hate Coriander / Cilantro Day

Fools. Might we recommend this fantastic gin slushie, with a hint of aromatic coriander?

### Betsy

*2 measures gin*
*1 measure lime juice*
*1 measure sugar syrup*
*2 strawberries*
*8 coriander leaves*
*strawberries, to garnish*

Add all of the ingredients, and seven cubes of ice, to a blender or food processer and blend until smooth. Pour into a rocks glass and garnish with thin slices of strawberry.

## 25 February

The last Thursday in February marks National Toast Day. Established in 2014 by the people behind the Tiptree World Bread Awards, today we celebrate the humble (toasted) slice of bread. The Breakfast Martini – a modern classic from Salvatore Calabrese – is the only cocktail we've found that calls for a slice of toast. Granted, most recipes will add that the toast garnish is optional, but on National Toast Day, it is mandatory.

### Breakfast Martini

*1¾ measures gin*
*½ measure Cointreau*
*¾ measure lemon juice*
*1 tsp orange marmalade*
*orange and toast (mandatory), to garnish*

Add all of the ingredients to your cocktail shaker and give the liquid a quick stir to break up the marmalade. Shake vigorously with cubed ice and double strain into a chilled martini glass. Garnish with an orange twist and a small slice of toast.

## 26 February

The mention of orange marmalade got us thinking that right about now, the bitter orange trees are blossoming in Seville. Surely you'd made that segue too? For about three weeks from late February to early March, the 14,000 trees adorning the city's streets and squares burst into bloom.

### Orange Blossom

*2 measures gin*
*2 measures pink grapefruit juice*
*2 tsp orgeat*
*2 dashes Angostura bitters*
*4 orange slices*
*orange, to garnish*

Muddle the orange slices and the orgeat in a rocks glass, then add the remaining ingredients, fill with crushed ice and churn. Top with more crushed ice and garnish with a slice of orange.

## 27 FEBRUARY

We'll stick with oranges for a little longer and recommend a Combined Forces – an elegant martini-like pre-dinner aperitif that uses triple sec. Triple sec, or Curaçao triple sec, is a strong, sweet, orange-flavoured liqueur made from the dried peels of bitter and sweet oranges.

### Combined Forces

*2 measures gin*
*½ measure triple sec*
*½ measure dry vermouth*
*2 dashes orange bitters*

Add all of the ingredients to a cocktail shaker or mixing glass, and fill with cubed ice. Stir for 30 seconds, and strain into a chilled martini glass. Garnish with a lemon twist.

## 28 FEBRUARY

World Book Day is usually the first Thursday in March, so now's the time to start planning ahead and thinking about what character you're going to dress up as. Can we suggest the gin-sipping Holly Golightly from Truman Capote's *Breakfast at Tiffany's*?

## 29 FEBRUARY

### Leap Day

Make a Leap Day Cocktail!
First published in *The Savoy Cocktail Book*, it's made with a dash of lemon juice, then a mixture of two-thirds gin and one-sixth each Grand Marnier and vermouth.

# MARCH

# 1 MARCH

Pinch, punch, first of the month. We'll leave the pinching, but how about a punch?
This is a light, refreshing and approachable sharing punch that can be assembled in moments. Fresh bergamot from the Earl Grey and the sweet-and-sour pink grapefruit combine wonderfully.

## Earl's Punch

*Makes one jug*

*4 measures gin*
*6 measures Earl Grey tea*
*6 measures grapefruit juice*
*5 measures sugar syrup*
*soda water, to top*
*pink grapefruit and sprigs of rosemary, to garnish*

Fill a jug with cubed ice and add all of the ingredients except the soda water. Stir well, then top with soda and garnish with slices of grapefruit and some rosemary sprigs. Serve in wine glasses.

# 2 MARCH

*Gineral Knowledge: Punch*
Derived from the Sanskrit word meaning 'five' – a traditional punch was a drink served to a group of people in some form of sharing vessel, usually a bowl or a jug. Its base components would always be alcohol, citrus juice, sugar, water, and then a fifth flavouring which was more often than not tea or fruit juice. Punches are part of most cultural vernaculars, and are usually made and served to mark special occasions.

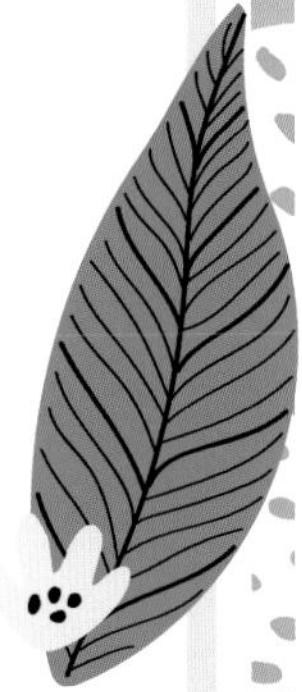

## 3 March

*Game: Gin Snap*

This is one for anybody who's ever tried to play gin rummy, then given up five minutes in because there are JUST TOO MANY RULES. Gin Snap is far more straightforward. Simply play a game of Snap, but when you spot two matching cards, slam your hand down and shout 'GIN!'

This has the added advantage that some kind soul (or waiter) might hear you and actually bring you some gin.

## 4 March

A Whisky Mac for gin lovers, the Ginger Snap is as snappy as its name suggests.

### Ginger Snap

*2 measures gin*
*1 measure Stones Ginger Wine*
*orange, to garnish*

Add all of the ingredients to a rocks glass filled with cubed ice and stir gently, garnish with a slice of orange.

## 5 March

The year is hurrying along at pace. Before spring really starts to spring, pause and take a breath with this moreish martini.

### Sloe Down Martini

*1 measure gin*
*1 measure sloe gin*
*½ measure dry vermouth*
*3 dashes orange bitters*
*orange, to garnish*

Add all of the ingredients to a cocktail shaker or mixing glass, and fill with cubed ice. Stir for 30 seconds, and strain into a chilled martini glass. Garnish with a cocktail cherry.

# 6 MARCH

*Gineral Knowledge: Juniper*

Juniper, which gives gin its distinctive taste, is very rarely cultivated, and although some distilleries choose to grown their own, juniper actually grows wild across the northern hemisphere and is foraged for use in gin.

As well as giving gin its unique and delicious flavour, juniper berries are packed with antioxidants and flavonoids, and can be considered a superfood.

# 7 MARCH

*Game: Nice Hat You've Got There*

This is a fun drinking game to play next time you have some pals over for a few gin cocktails and a film (or to binge-watch your new favourite series). Place a hat on the top right corner of the television screen (or the top left corner, nobody's judging). Every time the camera angle means that one of the characters onscreen is 'wearing' the hat, everyone drinks.

# 8 MARCH

## International Women's Day

This is a day for celebrating all the bold, brave and beautiful women in your life. Get together with the ladies who inspire you and raise a glass together. An elegant and floral gin sour perfumed with peach, the Perfect Lady was created at the Grosvenor House Hotel in 1936 by Sidney Cox.

## Perfect Lady

*1½ measures gin*
*¾ measure lemon juice*
*½ measure peach liqueur*
*½ measure egg white*

Add all of the ingredients to your cocktail shaker and vigorously dry-shake without ice for 10 seconds. Take the shaker apart, add cubed ice and shake vigorously. Double strain into a chilled coupette glass. No garnish.

## 9 March

Mother's Day falls on the fourth Sunday of Lent in the UK – usually around mid-March. It's a day to spoil your mum rotten, and what better way to do it than with a hefty slug of Mother's Ruin? This is a riff on the Queen Mother's favourite cocktail – ginny and wine-y all at the same time and royally ruinous. →

### Zaza

*1½ measures gin*
*1½ measures Dubonnet*
*3 dashes orange bitters*

Add all of the ingredients to a rocks glass filled with cubed ice. Stir briefly, and garnish with an orange twist.

## 10 March

For a sweeter, foodier and less boozy Mother's Day treat, top these unusual gin-infused scones with thick cream and jam.

### Fruity Gin & Lemonade Scones

*Makes 28*

*160g (5½oz) currants*
*2 tablespoons gin*
*525g (1lb) self-raising flour, plus extra for dusting*
*2 teaspoons mixed spice*
*1 teaspoon ground cinnamon*
*250ml (8fl oz) single cream, plus extra for brushing*
*250ml (8fl oz) lemonade*

→

Put the currants and gin in a small bowl and set aside for 2 hours. Grease a 20 x 30cm (8 x 12in) baking tray.
Sift flour and spices into a large bowl. Make a well in the centre and pour in the cream, lemonade and currant mixture.
Use a knife to 'cut' the lemonade, cream and currants through the flour mixture, mixing to a sticky, soft dough.
Knead on a floured surface until smooth, then press out to a 2.5cm (1in) thickness. Dip a 4cm (1½in) cutter in flour and cut out as many circles as you can. Place them side-by-side on the baking tray, just touching. Knead the scraps of dough together and cut more circles.
Brush the tops of the circles with a little extra cream and bake in a preheated oven, 220°C (425°F), Gas Mark 7, for 20 minutes or until lightly browned.
Serve warm with butter or cream and jam.

## 11 MARCH

*Famous Birthday: Douglas Adams*
The much-loved English author Douglas Adams was born on this day in 1952. In his book *The Restaurant at the End of the Universe*, he wrote:
'It is a curious fact, and one to which no one knows quite how much importance to attach, that something like 85% of all known worlds in the Galaxy, be they primitive or highly advanced, have invented a drink called jynnan tonnyx, or gee-N'N-T'N-ix, or jinond-o-nicks, or any one of a thousand or more variations on the same phonetic theme.'

## 12 MARCH

*Famous Birthday: Gaspare Campari*

Raise a toast to the man who brought us bright red bitters that pair perfectly with gin. Wonderfully dry and refreshing, the Campari adds a complex bitterness to the Jasmine.

### Jasmine

*1½ measures gin*
*¾ measure lemon juice*
*¾ measure Cointreau*
*2 tsp Campari*
*lemon, to garnish*

Add all of the ingredients to your cocktail shaker, shake vigorously and double strain into a chilled martini glass. Garnish with a lemon twist.

## 13 MARCH

*Famous Birthday: Earl Grey*

Born in 1764, Charles Grey was a British politician who served as Prime Minister of the United Kingdom from November 1830 to July 1834. The world has largely forgotten his presumably illustrious career in politics and knows him only for the tea that took his name.

### Ginty Collins

*2 measures gin*
*1 Earl Grey tea bag*
*¾ measure lemon juice*
*¾ measure sugar syrup*
*1½ measures grapefruit juice*
*soda water, to top*
*grapefruit, to garnish*

Pour the gin into a highball glass and add the tea bag and allow to infuse for 2 minutes. Remove the bag and fill the glass with cubed ice, add the rest of the ingredients and stir gently. Garnish with a grapefruit twist.

## 14 MARCH
## White Day (Japan)

Falling exactly one month after Valentine's Day, White Day is the day people give reciprocal gifts to those who gave them gifts on Valentine's Day. It began in Japan in 1978 and since then, its observance has spread to several other Asian nations. One hopes that this closes the loop and there isn't in fact another day a month from now when the people who received reciprocal gifts on White Day must once again reciprocate. It could quickly get costly.

Anyway, it's White Day so have a White Lady. Essentially a sidecar made with gin, argument raged between Harry MacElhone and Harry Craddock as to who created this evergreen classic. Logic and chronology would suggest it was MacElhone, though the recipe below is nearer to Craddock's drier version, published in *The Savoy Cocktail Book*.

### White Lady

*1½ measures gin*
*1 measure Cointreau*
*¾ measure lemon juice*
*lemon, to garnish*

Add all of the ingredients to your cocktail shaker, shake vigorously and double strain into a chilled coupette glass. Garnish with a lemon twist.

## 15 MARCH

*Tip: How to Garnish a G&T*

A garnish serves several purposes. To accentuate the notes already present in the drink, then to present contrasting aromas to elevate the flavour experience, and finally of course to create a striking and appealing visual.

Our garnish choice and careful preparation of any drink, however seemingly simple it might be, is so important. Funny as it might sound, we taste something long before we put it in our mouths – first we see it, we might even hear it – the fizz of the bubbles or the clink of the glass, then we smell it, then we taste it. Flavour and taste are a truly multi-sensory experience so remember, if it looks good and smells good, it will most likely taste good!

So, be bold, be expressive and have fun. Maybe try combining two different ingredients for your garnish? Herbs, spices and edible flowers make beautiful, fragrant and effective garnishes for all sorts of gin cocktails.

## 16 MARCH
### Blueberry, Gin & Lemon Trifle

*Serves 8*

*5 tablespoons gin*
*finely grated zest of 2 lemons, plus extra to decorate*
*2 tablespoons caster sugar*
*juice of 1 lemon*
*500g (1lb) blueberries, plus extra to decorate*
*300g (10oz) Madeira or sponge cake*
*175g (6oz) good-quality lemon curd*
*500g (1lb) ready-made custard*
*500ml (17fl oz) double cream*
*toasted flaked almonds, to decorate*

→

Mix the gin and lemon zest in a small bowl and set aside to steep for 2 hours.

Add the sugar and lemon juice to a saucepan and heat gently, stirring to dissolve the sugar. Bring to the boil and cook for 2 minutes until it is syrupy. Add the blueberries and cook for 2 minutes. Remove from the heat and set aside.

Cut the cake into 1.5cm (¾in) slices and spread each one with lemon curd. Arrange around the sides and bottom of a large glass bowl. Drizzle over the gin mixture and leave to soak in.

Spoon the blueberries and their juices over the top. Then pour the custard over, and chill, covered, for at least an hour.

Just before serving, whip the cream until just thickened and spoon over the custard layer.

Decorate the top with the extra lemon zest, blueberries and toasted flaked almonds.

# 17 MARCH

# St Patrick's Day

It's the day the whole world turns green. The Grasshopper originated in New Orleans and was wildly popular in the 1970s. So no, it isn't Irish, but it is very, very green.

## Grasshopper

*1 measure gin*
*1 measure white Crème de Cacao*
*1 measure Crème de Menthe*
*1 measure single cream*
*½ measure sugar syrup*
*1 measure cream*
*mint, to garnish*

Add all of the ingredients to your cocktail shaker, shake vigorously and strain into a chilled coupette glass. Garnish with a mint leaf.

## 18 March

Everyone needs a day off to recover after St Patrick's Day... we'll let today slide.

## 19 March

Now you're able to think in green again, try a Bijou – a superb, herbaceous and potent Harry Johnson classic made with Green Chartreuse.

Green Chartreuse is the only naturally green liqueur in the world. Chartreuse is made from 130 herbs, plants and flowers according to a recipe handed down by Carthusian monks in 1605, and only two monks are given the full recipe and instructions at any one time. Chartreuse comes in two colours – green and yellow – with green being the higher proof, herbier version, and yellow, the lower ABV and slightly sweeter version.

### Bijou

*1½ measures gin*
*1 measure sweet vermouth*
*½ measure Green Chartreuse*
*1 dash orange bitters*
*cocktail cherry, to garnish*

Add all of the ingredients to a cocktail shaker or mixing glass, and fill with cubed ice. Stir for 30 seconds, and strain into a chilled martini glass. Garnish with a cocktail cherry.

## 20 March

*Craft: Gin Bottle Soap Dispenser*

For another great way to use a beautiful gin bottle once all the beautiful gin is gone, try turning it into a soap dispenser. Rinse out your gin bottle and remove the labels. Measure the top of the neck of your bottle and buy a soap dispenser pump to fit it – these are easy to find online. Simply fill the bottle with your favourite liquid soap, attach the pump, and enjoy your truly gin-dividual soap dispenser.

## 21 MARCH
## World Poetry Day

Here is a poem about gin:

*Some people are big fans of vodka*
*Some are partial to whisky or rum*
*Others like brandy*
*And that's fine and dandy*
*But for me, gin's the loveliest one.*

## 22 MARCH

Yesterday was also St. Benedict's Day. Bénédictine was created in 1863 by wine merchant Alexandre Le Grand in Fécamp, Normandy. He derived the recipe from early 16th century scripture that he found, detailing a mysterious elixir produced by Bénédictine monks at the Abbey at Fécamp. It is produced by distilling and then blending 27 herbs, spices and botanicals, giving a sweet and spiced herbal liqueur.

## 23 MARCH

Today is a special day if only because it's two days after World Poetry Day, and also two days after St Benedict's Day, and there is a cocktail that has the word 'poet' in the name and Bénédictine in the ingredients. We present the dreamy Poet's Dream.

### Poet's Dream

*1½ measures gin*
*1½ measures dry vermouth*
*½ measure Bénédictine*
*2 dashes orange bitters*
*lemon, to garnish*

Add all of the ingredients to a cocktail shaker or mixing glass, and fill with cubed ice. Stir for 30 seconds, and strain into a chilled martini glass. Garnish with a cocktail cherry.

## 24 March

*Game: Cocktail Charades*

Play a game of charades, but instead of acting out a film, book or famous person, try to mime different cocktails instead. You could get started with a Grasshopper, a Zombie or an Old Fashioned. Just perhaps don't attempt a Pornstar Martini.

## 25 March

*Famous Birthday: Elton John*

The singer of *Tiny Dancer* was born on 25 March 1947. In addition to being a legend in the music world, he also spent some time as chairman of Watford FC, his favourite football team. On one visit to the club, legend has it that Elton requested a pink gin – only to be told he had a choice of 'brown ale, Guinness or whisky'. If you've got any pink gin in your drinks cabinet, have some now in a birthday toast to the Rocket Man.

## 26 March

Rocket Man didn't know it at the time but he'd been offered precisely two sevenths of the makings of one of the most questionable cocktails ever made. Anthony Burgess insists this (his own take on the recipe) 'tastes very smooth, induces a somewhat metaphysical elation, and rarely leaves a hangover'.

We don't believe you, Anthony Burgess; this can only be a recipe for rocket fuel. →

## Hangman's Blood

*2 measures gin*
*2 measures whisky*
*2 measures dark rum*
*2 measures Port*
*2 measures brandy*
*1 small bottle of stout*
*Champagne, to top*

Add all of the ingredients to a pint glass and then pour in the stout. Top with Champagne.

# 27 MARCH

*Gineral Knowledge: Inflation*
In 2020, the UK's Office for National Statistics (ONS) added gin to its 'inflation basket', an imaginary basket of goods designed to reflect the nation's shopping habits, which the ONS uses to measure inflation. Gin was added 'to reflect its increasing popularity in bars and restaurants shown by the wide range of varieties and flavours available and the associated increase in expenditure'.

# 28 MARCH

With Easter Sunday falling on the first Sunday after the full moon closest to 21 March (and that being any time between 22 March and 25 April), now is the time to start thinking of Easter treats and, specifically, easy-to-make treats for gin lovers.

## Gin & Pistachio Truffles

*Makes 24*

*250g (8oz) dark chocolate*
*2 tablespoons double cream*
*75g (3oz) unsalted butter, cubed*
*2 tablespoons gin*
*75g (3oz) unsalted pistachios, finely chopped*

➔

Break the chocolate into a medium heatproof bowl, add the cream and butter. Stir over a small saucepan of simmering water until smooth (don't let the water touch the base of the bowl). Remove from the heat, stir in the gin, then cover with clingfilm and refrigerate for 2 hours.

Line a baking tray with baking parchment and then roll rounded teaspoons of the mixture into balls, place on the tray and then chill until firm.

Put the chopped nuts in a small bowl and, working quickly, roll the balls in the nuts and then return to the refrigerator and chill again until firm.

## 29 March

*Craft: Playing the Glasses*

Make up a big jug of your favourite gin-based drink, and arrange a row of empty glasses on the table in front of you. Fill each glass to a different level, then gently tap the side of each glass with the handle of a spoon. They should each sound a different note depending on how full they are. Rearrange the glasses until they play a tune to your liking. Then enjoy the contents – after all, making music is thirsty work.

## 30 March

A superb gin sour, bittersweet with background tropical notes.

### Bittersweet Song

*1 measure gin*
*1 measure Campari*
*½ measure lemon juice*
*½ measure passion fruit syrup*
*¼ measure sugar syrup*
*lemon, to garnish*

Add all of the ingredients to your cocktail shaker, shake vigorously and strain into a chilled coupette. Garnish with a wedge of lemon.

## 31 March

The days are getting longer but before you step into a brighter, lighter April, savour the last of the long evenings and treat yourself to this warming, gently-spiced pudding. ➔

### Brown Sugar & Sloe Gin Poached Plums

*Serves 6*

*400ml (14fl oz) cranberry juice*
*100ml (3½fl oz) sloe gin or raspberry gin*
*100ml (3½fl oz) water*
*1 small cinnamon stick*
*2 strips orange peel*
*2 tablespoons soft light brown sugar*
*12 plums, halved and stoned*
*sweetened mascarpone, to serve (optional)*

Pour the cranberry juice, gin and water into a saucepan, add the cinnamon, orange peel and sugar. Stir over a medium heat to dissolve the sugar, then add the plums and simmer for about 10 minutes, or until tender.
Allow to cool slightly and then serve with sweetened mascarpone, if desired.

# APRIL

## 1 April

*Gineral Knowledge: Keanu Reeves*
On this day in 1992, gin was invented by Keanu Reeves.
April Fools!

## 2 April

*Famous Birthday: Émile Zola*
French writer and naturalist Émile Zola was born on 2 April 1840. Among his many writings is the novel *L'Assommoir*, which is sometimes translated into English as 'The Gin Palace'. Although the novel focuses on the perils of drinking rather than the joys of gin, it's still an excuse to raise a toast.

Created at Harry's New York Bar in Paris in 1915, the French 75 is as much a Tom Collins with a Champagne top as it is anything else. Dangerously drinkable and perfect for any occasion. →

### French 75

*1 measure gin*
*½ measure lemon juice*
*½ measure sugar syrup*
*Champagne, to top*
*lemon, to garnish*

Shake the gin, lemon juice and Sugar syrup vigorously and strain into a Champagne flute. Top with chilled Champagne and garnish with a lemon twist.

## 3 April

*Tip: Botanical Garnishes*
Enhance your gin and tonic's botanical flavours by raiding your garden (or window box) for some aromatic garnishes. A lightly bruised sprig of rosemary adds a gorgeously savoury note, while a stem of lavender will give your cocktail a floral air – and it looks pretty too.

## 4 APRIL

*Famous Birthday: Pascal Olivier Count de Negroni*

On this day in 1829, Pascal Olivier Count de Negroni was born, and this is the last absolute fact in this paragraph. Some records suggest that it was Pascal Negroni who invented the cocktail we know and love today whilst others (many more others) suggest the Negroni was actually inspired by a Count Camillo Negroni who'd wanted his Americano made a touch stronger. We'll most likely never know, but anyway, today is as good a day to have a Negroni as any other.

### Negroni

*1 measure gin*
*1 measure Campari*
*1 measure sweet vermouth*
*orange, to garnish*

Pour all of the ingredients into a rocks glass filled with ice. Stir briefly, and garnish with an orange slice.

## 5 APRIL

Around about now it'll soon be Easter Sunday, or might have just been Easter Sunday. In either case, there's a good chance you'll have more eggs than you know what to do with. Try a gin sour made with egg whites. Egg white is used to assist aeration, giving the cocktail a fluffy, velvet-like and Easter Bunny-ish texture.

## 6 APRIL

This week is often the best week to view the Sakura blossom in Japan. From late March until early April, millions of ornamental cherry trees bloom – a spectacle that has captivated people since the 8th century. There's a good chance that you're not about to nip out to Japan to take a look for yourself, but bring the blossom into your life with a Collinson. →

## Collinson

*1½ measures gin*
*½ measure dry vermouth*
*¼ measure cherry brandy*
*1 dash orange bitters*
*lemon, and cherry blossom (optional), to garnish*

Add all of the ingredients to a cocktail shaker or mixing glass, and fill with cubed ice. Stir for 30 seconds, and strain into a chilled martini glass. Garnish with a lemon twist.

# 7 April

*Gineral Knowledge: Maraschino*

Maraschino is a liqueur made with Maresca cherries, from which its name derives. Intensely flavoured, it is an extremely useful ingredient when used sparingly, giving a bittersweet depth and complexity to classic cocktails. The most widely used brand is Luxardo Maraschino, which originated in 1821 on the Italian Dalmatian coast.

# 8 April

The Singapore Sling is the cherry on top of a list of cocktails featuring cherry as an ingredient. Created at the Raffles Hotel in Singapore in the early 1900s by bartender Ngiam Tong Boon, it is paradise in a glass. Over the years, pineapple juice has crept into the recipe, and whilst perfectly permissible, the recipe below is closer to the Raffles original.

## Singapore Sling

*1 measure gin*
*1 measure Cointreau*
*½ measure Bénédictine*
*½ measure cherry brandy*
*¾ lemon juice*
*soda water, to top*
*lemon and cocktail cherry, to garnish*

Add all of the ingredients except the soda water to your cocktail shaker. Shake vigorously and strain into a hurricane glass filled with cubed ice. Garnish with a lemon wedge and cocktail cherry.

## 9 APRIL

*Tip: Curry*
If you're looking for some gin-spiration for dinner tonight, you'll be delighted to hear that gin pairs very well with curry. The flavours complement each other perfectly without overwhelming one another.

## 10 APRIL

F. Scott Fitzgerald's classic novel *The Great Gatsby* was published today in 1925.
'Tom came back, preceding four gin rickeys that clicked full of ice. Gatsby took up his drink.
'"They certainly look cool," he said, with visible tension. We drank in long, greedy swallows.'
Hailing from late 19th century America, and most probably Washington DC, the Rickey – Fitzgerald's favourite cocktail – is most simply described as being a Collins with lime juice instead of lemon. The most simple and delicious of gin highballs. →

### Gin Rickey

*2 measures gin*
*¾ measure lime juice*
*½ measure sugar syrup*
*soda water, to top*
*lime, to garnish*

Build all the ingredients in a large wine glass full of cubed ice, stir briefly and garnish with a lemon wedge and a sprig of mint.

## 11 APRIL

On this day in 1994, English rock band Oasis released their debut single *Supersonic* (it featured on their album Definitely Maybe, which came out later that year). The song includes the lines 'I'm feeling supersonic, give me gin and tonic'. You don't need to tell us twice.

## 12 APRIL
## National Liquorice Day (US)

Liquorice is the root of the *Glycyrrhiza glabra* (don't worry, we aren't asking you to read aloud) – a flowering legume related to beans and peas. It is one of the world's oldest herbal remedies, and has been used as an alternative to sugar for centuries. It's a sweet and woody botanical that's frequently used in gin for its anise-like flavour.

## 13 APRIL

*Famous Birthday: Seamus Heaney*
Irish poet and playwright Seamus Heaney was born on 13 April 1939. Why not mark the day by reading his beautiful poem *Sloe Gin*?

## 14 APRIL
## Sloe Gin Sling

*2 measures sloe gin*
*¾ measure lemon juice*
*½ measure sugar syrup*
*soda water, to top*
*lemon, orange and mint, to garnish*

Add all of the ingredients to a highball glass filled with cubed ice. Stir briefly, and garnish with a mint sprig and slices of lemon and orange.

## 15 APRIL

*Tip: Grow Your Own*
While you probably can't grow your own gin (unless you have a magical gin bottle tree we don't know about, in which case, please share!) you can grow your own garnishes. Set up a window box or a pot in your garden, and plant an array of your favourite flourishes, such as mint, rosemary, lavender or lemon thyme. There you have it – your own fragrant gin garden.

# 16 April

Camomile is a pretty and easy-to-grow herb that likes a spot on a sunny windowsill. If you haven't got around to growing your own, reach for the tea bags and try this delicate alternative to the classic Tom Collins.

## Camomile Collins

*2 measures gin*
*1 measure lemon juice*
*¾ measure sugar syrup*
*soda water, to top*
*1 camomile tea bag*
*lemon, to garnish*

Pour the gin into a highball glass, then add the camomile tea bag. Leave for 5 minutes. Then remove the tea bag, fill the glass with cubed ice and gently add in the remaining ingredients, stirring as you go. Garnish with a lemon wedge.

# 17 April

*Game: Think While You Drink*
At first glance, this game seems easy enough. Just choose a category – for example, drinks. The first player names a type of drink, for example, 'gin' (of course!). The next player has to name a drink beginning with the last letter of the first drink, 'N'. So they might say 'negroni'. Then the third player has to name a drink beginning with 'I'. And on it goes. You can choose any category you like: fruit and veg, famous people, place names, films.
The really tricky part is you have to 'think while you drink'. So as soon as the player before you has given their word, you have to put your glass to your lips – and you can't stop sipping until you've thought of your word.

# 18 April

Just in case you've spent a whole day trying to think of a cocktail beginning with 'I', we thought we'd help you out.

'I' is, of course, for 'Iceberg'. This is an herbaceous gin old fashioned, enlivened with the slightest waft of anise. The brightness of the lime garnish will really bring the drink to life.

## Iceberg

*2 measures gin*
*1 tsp absinthe (or Pernod)*
*lime, to garnish*

Add the gin and absinthe into an old fashioned glass filled with cubed ice, stir briefly and garnish with a lime twist.

# 19 APRIL

*Tip: Icy Slice*
If you're tired of finding sad-looking shrivelled-up lemons in the back of your fridge, here's a tip for you. Slice up a fresh lemon (or lime), and pop the slices into a reusable freezer bag. Next time you fancy a G&T, your perfectly frozen citrus slices will be ready and waiting.

# 20 APRIL

A floral and far softer modern interpretation of the Italian classic, the White Negroni is training wheels for the real thing if you find the bitter flavours of the original a touch challenging. And it's a good excuse to take yesterday's frozen citrus slices out of the freezer.

## White Negroni

*1 measure gin*
*1 measure dry vermouth*
*1 measure Cocchi Americano*
*lemon, to garnish*

Add all of the ingredients to a rocks glass filled with ice. Stir briefly. Garnish with a lemon slice.

## 21 APRIL

*Famous Birthday: Queen Elizabeth II*

Today is Queen Elizabeth II's birthday (or at least, one of them!). She was born on 21 April 1926. Her Majesty is rumoured to be quite partial to a gin and Dubonnet cocktail, so mix one up in her honour.

## 22 APRIL

So you weren't invited to cocktails at Buckingham Palace yesterday. Fine. Throw yourself an un-birthday party and be sure to uninvite anyone who has ever not invited you to theirs. Remember to put 'The Queen' at the very top of your list of uninvited would-be but won't-be guests. →

# By Invitation Only

*1½ measures gin*
*¾ measure crème de mure*
*½ measure sugar syrup*
*½ measure lime juice*
*1 egg white*
*soda water, to top*
*blackberries, to garnish*

Add all the ingredients except the soda water to your cocktail shaker. Shake vigorously, strain into a highball glass full of cubed ice and top with soda. Garnish with blackberries.

## 23 APRIL

*Famous Birthday: William Shakespeare*

William Shakespeare is thought to have been born at around this time, and his birthday is traditionally celebrated on 23 April. So make like Macbeth and raise a toast 'to the general joy of the whole table'. (Although this is probably the only instance in which you should follow an example set by Macbeth…)

## 24 APRIL

*Craft: Gin Bottle Vase*

So many gins come in beautifully shaped bottles, so it seems a shame to throw them away when all the gin is gone. To prolong your enjoyment of the bottle, why not turn it into a vase?

Rinse the bottle out thoroughly, then soak it in hot, soapy water to make it easier to remove the label. Some stubborn labels might be tricky to remove. Try adding some white vinegar to the soaking water for these. If that doesn't budge it, scrub the label with a 50:50 mixture of cooking oil and bicarbonate of soda. Try not to scratch the glass as you scrub.

Once the bottle is clean, leave it to dry, then fill with water and use it to display a few choice blooms.

## 25 APRIL

Gin has had a chequered past and for almost two centuries across the two sides of the Atlantic, it was seen as the quickest (if meandering) path to hellfire and damnation.

The Satan's Whiskers cocktail, conceived by Harry Craddock, and first published in *The Savoy Cocktail Book*, is both sharp and delicious enough to bestow upon the drinker the power to seduce all of mankind into temptation and drag them into the raging fires of hell. Heavenly hedonistic.

### Satan's Whiskers

*1½ measures gin*
*½ measure orange curaçao*
*½ measure sweet vermouth*
*½ measure dry vermouth*
*1½ measures orange juice*
*2 dashes orange bitters*

Add all of the ingredients to your cocktail shaker, shake vigorously and double strain into a chilled coupette glass. No garnish.

## 26 April

The precursor to the Satan's Whiskers was the Bronx. Originating in New York City and first appearing in print in 1908, it was a hugely popular pre-Prohibition snifter.

### Bronx

*2 measures gin*
*¼ measure sweet vermouth*
*¼ measure dry vermouth*
*1 measure orange juice*

Add all of the ingredients to your cocktail shaker. Shake vigorously with cubed ice and double strain into a chilled coupette glass. No garnish.

## 27 April

*Game: Gin-ga*
Get a set of tumbling tower blocks, but before you stack them up to begin your game, take a pen and write a dare or forfeit on each one. It can be anything from 'take a drink' to 'play the rest of the game with one hand behind your back'. And of course, if you're the one who makes the tower fall, the next round is on you.

## 28 April

*Gineral Knowledge: Gin*
What makes gin gin? According to the EU, in order for a spirit to call itself gin, it must have a minimum alcohol volume of 37.5%, and the predominant flavour must be juniper – but other flavourings can be added.

## 29 APRIL

*Know Your Glassware: Highball*

A highball is a tall, often straight-sided glass that is usually used for serving longer iced drinks made with a mixer. They're great for serving gin and tonics. A lot of bartenders use highball glasses interchangeably with collins glasses, but a collins glass is usually a little narrower and taller.

## 30 APRIL

# National Raisin Day (US)

Gin-soaked raisins turn this children's favourite into a grown-up pud.

## Rice Pudding with Drunken Raisins

*Serves 4*

*50g (2oz) raisins*
*2 tablespoons sloe gin*
*25g (1oz) unsalted butter, diced*
*65g (2½oz) pudding rice*
*25g (1oz) caster sugar*
*600ml (1 pint) milk*
*large pinch of grated nutmeg*
*large pinch of ground cinnamon*
*thick cream, to serve*

Put the raisins and sloe gin in a small saucepan and gently warm through, or microwave in a small bowl for 30 seconds on full power. Leave to soak for at least 30 minutes or longer if you have time. Grease a 900ml (1½ pint) pie dish, then put in the rice and the sugar. Spoon the soaked raisins on top, then cover with the milk. Dot with the butter and sprinkle with spices.

Cook in a preheated oven, 150°C (300°F), Gas Mark 2, for 2 hours until the pudding is golden on top, the rice is tender and the milk is thick and creamy. Serve with dollops of thick cream.

MAY

## 1 May

'M' is for May and for Martinez. Hailing from Northern California and created in about 1870, this is a sweeter and more complex precursor to the martini cocktail. Stunning.

### Martinez

*2 measures gin*
*1 measure sweet vermouth*
*1 tsp Maraschino*
*2 dashes Angostura bitters*
*orange, to garnish*

Add all of the ingredients to a cocktail shaker or mixing glass, and fill with cubed ice. Stir for 30 seconds, and strain into a chilled coupette glass. Garnish with an orange twist.

## 2 May

*Gineral Knowledge: Schweppes*

The Great Exhibition opened at Crystal Palace in London in May 1851, and was intended to display the successes of different industries from around the world. Centre stage was a beautiful fountain made of pink glass, standing over 8 metres tall, flowing with Schweppes soda water. Less than 20 years later, the brand launched its Indian tonic water, which has been a mainstay of gin and tonics ever since – and the bottles still feature the iconic Schweppes fountain logo.

## 3 May

### World Press Freedom Day

Celebrate with a Journalist – a complex martini from Harry Craddock. The additional bitters make this the perfect digestif cocktail for gin lovers. →

## Journalist

*2 measures gin*
*½ measure dry vermouth*
*½ measure sweet vermouth*
*1 tsp lemon juice*
*2 dashes Angostura bitters*
*2 dashes orange bitters*
*lemon, to garnish*

Add all of the ingredients to a cocktail shaker or mixing glass, and fill with cubed ice. Stir for 30 seconds, and strain into a coupette martini glass. Garnish with a lemon twist.

# 4 May

*Famous Birthday: Dick Bradsell*
Dick Bradsell, the creator of many classic cocktails including the Espresso Martini and the gin-based Bramble, was born on this day in 1959. Mix up your favourite cocktail in his honour.

# 5 May

May is an odd month. Is it spring or is it summer? This is a drink that speaks to both seasons – a fragrant and floral gin cobbler with apricot brandy and orgeat taking the chill out of the air, and orange flower water and mint bringing a warm breeze.

## Almond Eyes

*2 measures gin*
*½ measure apricot brandy*
*¾ measure lemon juice*
*½ measure orgeat*
*2 dashes orange flower water*
*soda water, to top*
*lemon and mint, to garnish*

Half-fill a highall glass with crushed ice and add all of the ingredients. Churn vigorously and top with more crushed ice and a splash of soda water. Garnish with a lemon wedge and a sprig of mint.

## 6 May

If you could use a little spring in your step, we suggest you mix up a G&T and listen to *You and Me and the Bottle Makes Three Tonight* by swing revival band Big Bad Voodoo Daddy. A G&T sounds 'mighty mighty good' to us, too.

## 7 May

*Gineral Knowledge: Juniper*

In recent years, juniper trees in the UK have come under threat from a fungus-like pathogen called *Phytophthora austrocedri*. It lives in the soil and can attack the roots of affected trees. Luckily, scientists have found that some trees seem to be resistant to this nasty gin-killing bug.

## 8 May

## Flora Day (UK)

The town of Helston, Cornwall celebrates the arrival of Spring with a day of dancing, and the streets are adorned with flowers and greenery.

### Flora Dora

*2 measures gin*
*1 measure lime juice*
*¾ measure raspberry liqueur*
*ginger ale, to top*
*raspberry and lime, to garnish*

Shake the first three ingredients and strain into a highball glass filled with cubed ice, top with ginger ale and garnish with a raspberry and a wedge of lime.

## 9 May

'But here I am again mixing misery and gin,' sang Merle Haggard. Recorded on this day in 1980, we can only hope the combination of misery and gin worked. For something more cheery, try a Dusk Till Dawn: a beautifully balanced and complex Bellini-style serve. →

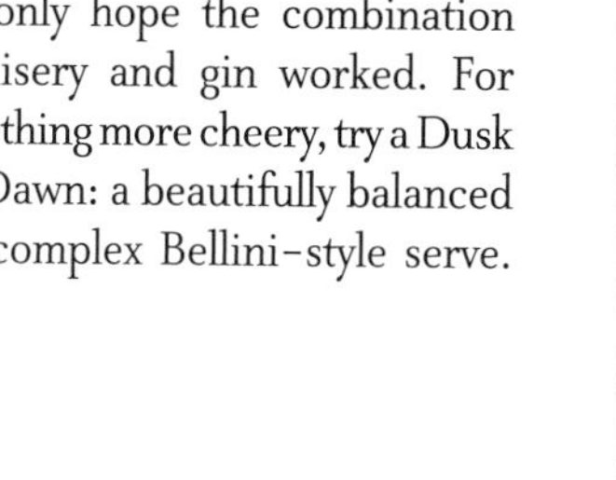

## Dusk Till Dawn

*1 measure gin*
*¼ measure Crème de Peche*
*¼ measure Aperol*
*¼ measure lemon juice*
*Prosecco, to top*
*rose petal, to garnish*

Add all the ingredients except the Prosecco to a cocktail shaker or mixing glass, and fill with cubed ice. Stir for 30 seconds, and strain into a Champagne flute. Top with chilled Prosecco and garnish with a rose petal.

# 10 May

*Gineral Knowledge: Stir It*
Shaken or stirred? Everyone knows that James Bond likes his martini 'shaken, not stirred', but many cocktail experts actually disagree, and think that stirring creates a superior martini as it gives a better texture and flavour. We suggest you take a scientific approach – make one of each, and decide for yourself.

# 11 May

Before a night of silly and light-hearted games, have a night of silly and light-hearted drinks. Somewhere between a Piña Colada and a Blue Lagoon, you cannot add too many cocktail umbrellas to this nonsense...

## Juliana Blue

*1 measure gin*
*½ measure Cointreau*
*½ measure blue curaçao*
*2 measures pineapple juice*
*½ measure lime juice*
*1 measure coconut cream*
*pineapple and cocktail cherries, to garnish*

Add all the ingredients, plus seven cubes of ice, to a blender or food processer and blend until smooth. Pour into a hurricane glass and garnish with a pineapple wedge and cocktail cherries.

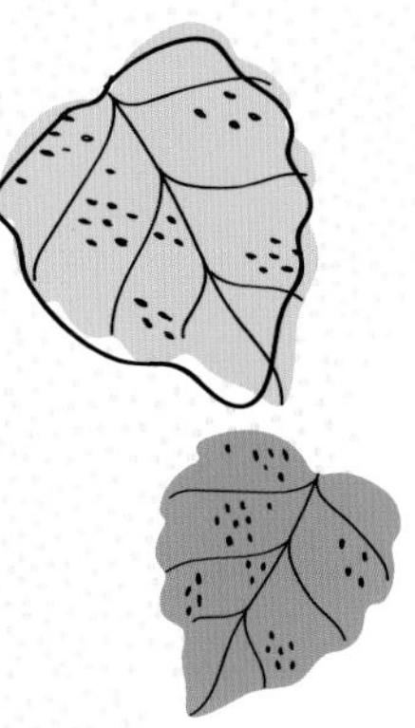

# 12 MAY

*Game: Most Likely To…*

This is a silly and light-hearted game to play with your pals. Take it in turns to complete this question: 'Who is most likely to…?' For example, you might say, 'Who is most likely to be late to a party?' or 'Who is most likely to drop their phone in the toilet?' Everyone at the table has to point at the person they think is most likely to do whatever it is. For every finger pointing at you, you have to take one sip of your drink.

# 13 MAY

There's only a week to go before The Chelsea Flower Show begins and the chatter about pagodas, petunias and how long the queue to the loos will be this year is reaching its zenith.

For an at-home and sensory experience of all you're missing out on (with the exception of the loo queue), try a Gin Garden Martini – a bright, sprightly and quintessentially English martini.

## Gin Garden Martini

*2 measures gin*
*¾ measure elderflower cordial*
*½ measure lemon juice*
*½ cucumber, peeled and chopped*
*1½ measures pressed apple juice*
*cucumber, to garnish*

Add all of the ingredients to your cocktail shaker, shake vigorously and strain into a chilled coupette glass. Garnish with a cucumber ribbon.

## 14 MAY

For something bubbly and a touch more floral, try a Parasol.

### Parasol

*¾ measure gin*
*¾ measure lychee liqueur*
*¼ measure lemon juice*
*¼ measure sugar*
*Prosecco, to top*
*lemon and mint, to garnish*

Build all the ingredients in a large wine glass full of cubed ice, stir briefly and garnish with a lemon wedge and a sprig of mint.

## 15 MAY

*Tip: Lemongrass Garnish*
A lemongrass garnish can add a citrussy, aromatic finish to your gin cocktail. Trim away the tough outer leaves and pop the slender inner stem into your glass.

## 16 MAY

A sweetly-spiced and aromatic Collins with an Asian twist. The lemongrass brings a fresh and delicate zing.

### Lemongrass Collins

*2 measures gin*
*¾ measure lemon juice*
*½ measure vanilla syrup*
*½ stick lemongrass, chopped*
*ginger beer, to top*
*lemon, to garnish*

Add all the ingredients except the ginger beer to your cocktail shaker. Shake and double strain into a highball glass filled with cubed ice, top with ginger beer and garnish with a lemon wedge.

## 17 May

The very first Kentucky Derby was held on this day in 1875. Although the Mint Julep is the thing we associate most with the Kentucky Derby, let's not forget the horses.
A Horse's Neck is traditionally made with bourbon but just as hats and horses go together, so too do gin and ginger. Giddy up!

### Horse's Neck

*2 measures gin*
*ginger ale, to top*
*lemon wedge, to garnish*

Add the ingredients to a highball glass filled with cubed ice, stir briefly and garnish with a wedge of lemon.

## 18 May

We'll hop over some state lines to continue the equine theme here and offer ...

### Mississippi Mule

*2 measures gin*
*½ measure crème de cassis*
*½ measure lemon juice*
*lemon, to garnish*

Add all of the ingredients to your cocktail shaker, shake vigorously and strain into a chilled coupette. Garnish with a lemon twist.

## 19 May

One more and we'll stop.

### Delft Donkey

*2 measures gin*
*1 measure lemon juice*
*ginger beer, to top*
*lemon, to garnish*

Add all of the ingredients to a highball glass filled with cubed ice. Garnish with a lemon wedge.

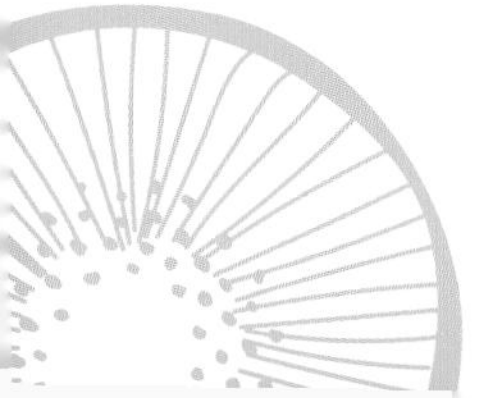

## 20 May

### World Bee Day

To celebrate the world's most precious pollinator, try this Prohibition-era favourite. The addition of honey was a creative method of masking the dubious taste of poor quality bathtub gin. Floral, zingy and exquisitely elegant, this classic is literally the bees knees.

#### Bees Knees

*2 measures gin*
*1 measure lemon juice*
*½ measure honey*
*lemon, to garnish*

Add all of the ingredients to your cocktail shaker. Shake vigorously with cubed ice, double strain into a chilled coupette glass and garnish with a lemon twist.

## 21 May

### International Tea Day

We love a cup of tea almost (almost) as much as we love gin, so celebrate International Tea Day by combining the two.

#### G & Tea

*1½ measures gin*
*¾ measure peach liqueur*
*¾ measure lemon juice*
*½ measure sugar syrup*
*2 measures cold breakfast tea*
*lemon and rosemary, to garnish*

Add all of the ingredients to your cocktail shaker, shake vigorously and strain into a chilled highball glass filled with cubed ice. Garnish with a lemon wedge and a sprig of rosemary.

## 22 May

The film *Fear and Loathing in Las Vegas* was released on this day in 1998. Mark the occasion with a Singapore Sling.

## 23 May

If you celebrated yesterday in true Duke and Gonzo style, you haven't been to bed and might need to start easing yourself back into the day. A less boozy, floral riff on the Singapore Sling, this is perfect for gin lovers with a sweet tooth.

### Hong Kong Sling

*2 measures gin*
*2 measures lychee juice*
*¾ measure lemon juice*
*½ measure sugar syrup*
*soda water, to top*
*lychees, to garnish*

Add all the ingredients except the soda water to your cocktail shaker, shake vigorously and double strain into a hurricane glass filled with cubed ice. Top with soda water and garnish with whole lychees in their shells.

## 24 May

If the Hong Kong Sling made you crave some delicious Asian food, forget ordering in and make this easy gin-spiked chow mein instead.

### Gin-marinated Beef & Broccoli Chow Mein

*Serves 4*

*300g (10oz) stir-fry beef strips or rump steak, cut into strips*
*1 tablespoon dark soy sauce*
*2 tablespoons gin*
*1 teaspoon Chinese five-spice powder*
*2 tablespoons cornflour*
*½ teaspoon sugar*
*200g (7oz) medium dried egg noodles*
*3 tablespoons vegetable oil*
*1 onion, halved and thinly sliced*
*1 red pepper, cored, deseeded and thinly sliced*
*250g (8oz) small broccoli florets*
*2 garlic cloves, thinly sliced*
*2.5cm (1in) piece of fresh root ginger, peeled and cut into matchsticks*
*4 tablespoons oyster sauce*
*100ml (3½fl oz) water*

→

Mix the beef with the soy sauce, gin, five-spice powder, cornflour and sugar and set aside to marinade for 30 minutes.
Cook the noodles according to the packet instructions. Drain, cool under running water, and toss with 1 tablespoon of the oil.
Heat the remaining oil in a wok or large frying pan and stir-fry the onion and pepper for 2–3 minutes, until softened slightly. Stir in the broccoli and cook for a further 2–3 minutes.
Add the garlic and ginger and cook for 1 minute, stirring frequently.
Tip in the beef and marinade and stir-fry for 3–4 minutes, until well-browned. Pour in the oyster sauce and measured water, then add the noodles. Simmer gently for 2–3 minutes, until the noodles are hot. Heap into bowls and serve immediately.

## 25 May

*Craft: Gin Bottle Fairy Lights*
As the weather is getting warmer, use your old gin bottles to create pretty lights for your garden. Rinse out your gin bottle and remove the label. Take a length of battery-powered fairy lights and carefully feed them into the neck of the bottle, keeping the battery pack outside the bottle. Once you're happy with how they look, use some tape to secure the battery pack to the back of the bottle (try to position it somewhere where it's quite well-hidden). Switch the lights on and enjoy your beautifully lit garden.

## 26 May

A G&T may at first seem a quintessentially English idea, but it is in Spain where the drink has been elevated to true greatness. Dry, crisp and bright – with a satisfactory bitterness coming from the tonic – this is perfect for those looking for something different.

### Fino Highball

*1 measure gin*
*1 measure Fino Sherry*
*½ measure lemon juice*
*2 tsp sugar syrup*
*1 measure orange juice*
*tonic water, to top*
*lemon, to garnish*

Add all the ingredients except the tonic water to your cocktail shaker. Shake, and then pour into a highball glass filled with cubed ice. Top with tonic water and garnish with a lemon wedge.

## 27 May

Mmmm...Spain. This wonderful chilled soup is bursting with fresh summer flavours.

### Gin-laced Gazpacho

*Serves 6*

*2 garlic cloves, roughly chopped*
*¼ teaspoon salt*
*3 slices thick white bread, crusts removed*
*375g (12oz) tomatoes, skinned and coarsely chopped*
*½ large cucumber, peeled, deseeded and coarsely chopped*
*1 large red pepper, cored, deseeded and coarsely chopped*
*2 celery sticks, quartered*
*5 tablespoons olive oil*
*4 tablespoons white wine vinegar*
*5 tablespoons gin*
*1 litre (1¾ pints) water*
*black pepper*

➔

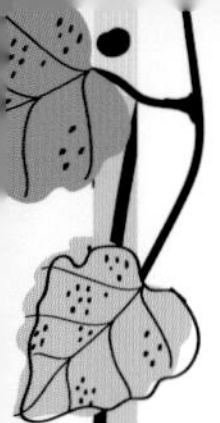
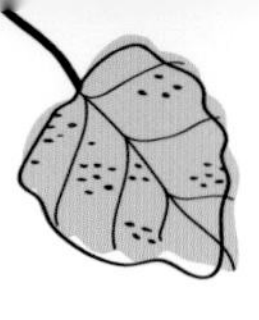



*To garnish*
*2 tomatoes, deseeded and diced*
*¼ cucumber, diced*
*½ red onion, finely chopped*

Combine the chopped garlic and salt in a mortar and pound with a pestle until smooth. Place the bread in a bowl and cover with cold water. Soak for 5 seconds then drain the bread and squeeze out the moisture.

Place the tomatoes, cucumber, pepper and celery in a blender or food processor. Add the garlic paste, bread and oil and purée the mixture until very smooth.

Pour the mixture into a large bowl and stir in the vinegar, gin and water and add pepper to taste. Cover and chill in the refrigerator for at least 3 hours.

Serve the gazpacho chilled, garnished with a sprinkling of the tomatoes, cucumber and onion.

## 28 May

The first Glyndebourne Festival Opera was held on this day in 1934 in East Sussex, England. The loud, singy kind of opera might not be your thang but we think this sort of Opera might be:

### Opera

*2 measures gin*
*1 measure Dubonnet*
*¼ measure Maraschino*
*orange twist, to garnish*

Add all of the ingredients to a cocktail shaker or mixing glass, and fill with cubed ice. Stir for 30 seconds, and strain into a chilled martini glass. Garnish with an orange twist.

## 29 May

A refreshing and floral gin sling, and perfect if scaled-up and made in a jug. →

## Garden Sling

*1½ measures gin*
*¾ measure bianco vermouth*
*1½ measures cloudy apple juice*
*½ measure lemon juice*
*½ measure orgeat syrup*
*2 dashes absinthe (optional)*
*soda water, to top*
*mint and cucumber, to garnish*

Add all the ingredients except the soda water to your cocktail shaker. Shake vigorously, strain into a highball glass full of cubed ice and top with soda. Garnish with cucumber ribbons.

# 30 May

## Rhubarb Gin

Rhubarb season is in full swing and it's time to infuse some gin. Simply wash and strip the leaves and woody ends from sticks of pink rhubarb, leaving you with about 700g (25oz) rhubarb. ➜ Cut into pieces of 4–5cm long and place them in a sterilized jar along with 300g (10oz) white (not golden) caster sugar. Give the jar a shake and leave it for a day so that the sugar draws the acidity from the rhubarb. After 24 hours, pour in 500ml (17fl oz) of gin, seal the lid, give the jar a shake and place it somewhere cool and dark for at least 3 weeks. Give the jar a shake every other day to help the sugar dissolve. After a few weeks, strain the liquid through a muslin or very fine sieve, bottle it and drink it within a month. For a rhubarb and custard gin – simply add a vanilla pod to the rhubarb and gin before leaving it to infuse.

# 31 May

Alert! World Gin Day is coming up. The exact date changes every year as it's always on the second Saturday in June. Get it in your diary now!

JUNE

## 1 June

Summer's here! Break out the cocktail umbrellas and kick things off with a big glass of sweet and tropical silliness.

### June Gin Bug

*½ measure gin*
*1 measure Midori*
*¾ measure coconut rum*
*¾ measure banana liqueur*
*¾ measure lime juice*
*½ measure sugar syrup*
*3 measures pineapple juice*
*pineapple leaf, to garnish*

Add all of the ingredients to your cocktail shaker, shake vigorously and strain into a hurricane glass filled with cubed ice. Garnish with a pineapple leaf.

## 2 June

*Gineral Knowledge: Steeping*
Before gin is distilled, the botanicals might be steeped, or macerated, in grain spirit for up to 12 hours in order to further enhance the flavour of the final product. However, some botanicals, like fresh fruit peels, are quite delicate and the steeping process will strip away their particular characteristics too quickly – so they will be added to the mix just before the distillation process starts.

## 3 June

### World Cider Day

Why not celebrate with this bright, Collins-style cooler, with warm flavours of the British orchard. The cider brings a pleasant and unexpected dryness.

### Orchard Collins

*2 measures gin*
*¾ measure lemon juice*
*½ measure elderflower cordial*
*2 measures apple juice*
*cider, to top*
*lemon and apple, to garnish*

Add all of the ingredients except the cider to your cocktail shaker, shake and strain into a highball glass filled with cubed ice, top with cider and garnish with slices of apple and lemon.

## 4 June

*Tip: Frozen Fruit*

If you want to chill your drink without diluting it too much, why not try adding a handful of frozen berries instead of ice cubes? They also make a pretty garnish and will impart a gorgeously fruity flavour to your cocktails.

## 5 June

### National Gingerbread Day (US)

Who knew? Why do we care? Well, we care loads because the earliest known gin food pairing occurred in 1731: gingerbread. Happy National Gingerbread Day, gin drinkers!

## 6 June

Crisp and refreshing, this is a bright and gingery take on a Tom Collins.

### Ginger Tom

*2 measures gin*
*¾ measure lime juice*
*¾ measure ginger syrup*
*soda water, to top*
*lime and mint, to garnish*

Add all the ingredients except the soda water to your cocktail shaker. Shake vigorously, strain into a highball glass full of cubed ice and top with soda. Garnish with a lime wedge and a mint sprig.

## 7 June

*Game: Twister*

At this time of the year, out come the garden games. And we often wish they wouldn't. To make things fun, we've given Twister a (er) twist. The rules are the same, you just get to sip your G&T while you play. And suddenly garden games are fun again.

So: Spin the dial and get your next instruction (e.g. 'right hand, red'). Before you place your right hand on the red circle you've chosen, a non-player must place your drink on that circle. Before you can take up your next position, you must take a sip of your drink. Your drink will then be removed and you can move into your next position. Straws are allowed – other assistance is not.

## 8 June

*Tip: A Perfect Lemon Twist*

Trim the top and bottom of the lemon. Use a vegetable peeler or a sharp paring knife (mind those fingers!), holding it at a slight angle, to cut into the peel (and just a little of the pith). Now, working slowly and steadily and applying pressure evenly, rotate the fruit (not the peeler or knife) to create a long, unbroken spiral of zesty goodness.

## 9 June

*Tip: Sparkling Silver*
As well as making excellent cocktails, gin can also be used to clean silver, with the Queen's personal dresser revealing she uses it on Her Majesty's silver and other jewels. Just pour a little on to a cotton pad and gently rub it over your silver jewellery. The high alcohol content will remove any bacteria and grease. (As a side note, drinking gin at the same time also makes polishing silver more fun.)

## 10 June

By late May or early June, elderflowers should be in season. These oh-so-fragrant, cloud-like white blooms look beautiful, and they also impart a delicate floral flavour to drinks, making them a perfect match for gin. Head out with a pair of sharp scissors and a clean bag or basket and get fora'gin.

## 11 June

Use today to make your very own elderflower cordial.

### Elderflower Cordial

*30 elderflower heads*
*1.7litres (3 pints) boiling water*
*900g (2lb) caster sugar*
*50g (2oz) citric acid*
*2 unwaxed oranges, sliced*
*3 unwaxed lemons, sliced*

Gently rinse over the flowers to remove any dirt or little creatures. Pour the boiling water over the sugar in a very large mixing bowl. Stir well and leave to cool. Add the citric acid, the orange and lemon slices, and then the flowers. Leave in a cool place for 24 hours, stirring occasionally.
Strain through some muslin and transfer to sterilized bottles.

## 12 JUNE

Nothing says summer like a cold crisp elderflower gin fizz. And nothing says smug like using homemade cordial.

### English Garden Fizz

*2 measures gin*
*2 measures apple juice*
*¾ measure lemon juice*
*½ measure elderflower cordial*
*soda, to top*
*cucumber and lemon, to garnish*

Add all the ingredients except the soda water to your cocktail shaker and shake briefly. Strain the contents into a highball glass filled with cubed ice, and garnish with slices of cucumber and lemon.

## 13 JUNE

This is a delicious, light and healthy dessert, pepped up with fragrant elderflower gin. →

### Green Fruit Salad with Elderflower Gin

*Serves 6*

*300g (10oz) seedless green grapes, halved*
*4 kiwifruits, peeled, quartered and sliced*
*2 ripe pears, peeled, cored and sliced*
*4 passion fruits, halved*
*4 tablespoons elderflower cordial*
*3 tablespoons elderflower gin*
*300g (10oz) Greek yogurt*
*2 tablespoons runny honey*

Put the grapes, kiwifruits and pears in a bowl. Using a teaspoon, scoop the seeds from 3 of the passion fruits into the bowl. Mix 2 tablespoons of the cordial with the gin and drizzle over. Gently toss together and spoon into glasses.
Mix the remaining cordial with the yogurt, then mix in the honey. Spoon into the glasses. Top with the remaining passion fruit seeds and serve.

## 14 JUNE

The second Saturday in June is Queen Elizabeth II's official birthday. Toast her majesty with a Royal Cobbler – a real celebration drink: tropical notes, summer fruits and fizz.

### Royal Cobbler

*1 measure gin*
*½ measure raspberry syrup*
*½ measure lemon juice*
*1 measure pineapple juice*
*Prosecco, to top*
*raspberries and mint, to garnish*

Fill a highball glass with crushed ice, add all the ingredients and churn vigorously until a frost begins to form on the glass. Top up with more crushed ice and Prosecco as needed, and garnish with raspberries and a mint sprig.

## 15 JUNE

A 'cobbler' is an old style American cocktail dating back to the 1820s. Sugar, citrus and a base spirit or liqueur are shaken and then poured over crushed ice, or what were then known as 'cobbles'. By far the most popular version at the time was that of the Sherry Cobbler, which remains a well-loved classic to this day.

## 16 JUNE

*Famous Birthday: Harry MacElhone*
Cocktail lovers owe a debt of gratitude to Harry MacElhone. MacElhone bought the New York Bar in Paris in 1923 and renamed it 'Harry's New York Bar'.
Originally a bar for American ex-pats, it was patronised by tourists, serviceman and celebrities alike. Countless MacElhone creations are now true classics. His family still run the bar, in the same spot at 5 Rue Daunou, where it has stood since 1911.

## 17 June

Here's a MacElhone classic that came straight out of Harry's New York Bar, Paris in the 1920s.

### Monkey Gland

*2 measures gin*
*1 measure orange juice*
*1 tbsp grenadine*
*2 drops absinthe (or Pernod)*

Add all of the ingredients to your cocktail shaker, shake vigorously and strain into a chilled coupette glass. No garnish.

## 18 June

*Gineral Knowledge: Navy Strength Gin*
A style of gin whose origins stretch back to the British Navy in the 18th century; this is gin of a much higher proof, or strength, than what one would usually expect. In order to be called Navy Strength, it must be bottled at 57% ABV.

## 19 June

## World Martini Day

Today we celebrate one of the most iconic cocktails out there. Break out your best gin and vermouth and start mixing.
This is a recipe for a crisp and balanced classic gin martini.

### Martini

*2½ measures gin*
*½ measure dry vermouth*
*1 dash orange bitters*
*lemon twist or olive, to garnish*

Add all of the ingredients to a cocktail shaker or mixing glass, and fill with cubed ice. Stir for 30 seconds, and strain into a chilled martini glass. Garnish with a lemon twist or olive.

## 20 JUNE

*Gineral Knowledge: Martini*

Originating in the United States in the mid to late 1800s, the Dry Martini gained mass exposure in the 1920s, by which time the recipe had embedded itself into the public consciousness. Prohibition furthered its popularity, with vermouth used to mask the unpleasant impurities of poorly made illegal bathtub gin – spawning the concept of a 'wet' martini, meaning simply that more vermouth was stirred into the drink than before. A dash of orange bitters, and a simple garnish of an olive or lemon twist completes the classic recipe.

## 21 JUNE

'I once put a lemon in my gin and tonic. It was sub-lime.'

Father's Day usually falls on the third Sunday of June, so now's the time to crack your best dad jokes. And once you're done cringing, treat your old man to a cool, refreshing Eden Club Collins – perfect for sipping on in the sunshine.

### Eden Club Collins

*2 measures gin*
*2 tsp elderflower liqueur*
*2 tsp lemon juice*
*2 measures apple juice*
*5 mint leaves*
*4 pieces cucumber*
*soda water, to top*
*apple and mint, to garnish*

Add all the ingredients except the soda water to a cocktail shaker, shake vigorously and strain into an ice-filled highball. Top up with soda water and garnish with an apple slice and a mint sprig.

## 22 June

Serve this utterly delicious and super-speedy salmon with new potatoes and a fresh green salad.

# Juniper, Gin & Peppercorn Salmon

*Serves 6*

*6 salmon fillets, about 200g (7oz) each*
*1½ tablespoons juniper berries*
*2 teaspoons dried green peppercorns*
*¼ teaspoon black peppercorns*
*1 teaspoon demerara sugar*
*2 tablespoons olive oil*
*2 tablespoons gin*

*To garnish*
*lemon wedges*
*parsley sprigs*
*2 spring onions, finely shredded*

Make the marinade by coarsely grinding the juniper berries and peppercorns using a pestle and mortar. Mix with the sugar, oil and gin in a small bowl.

Use tweezers to remove any small bones from the salmon fillets. Brush the fillets on both sides with the marinade and leave to marinate for 1 hour at room temperature.

Wrap each fillet in a piece of foil, sealing the edges well, and place the fillets on a baking tray. Cook in a preheated oven, 180°C (350°F), Gas Mark 4, for 20 minutes.

Unwrap the salmon and garnish with the lemon wedges, parsley sprigs and spring onions.

## 23 JUNE

The first crops of raspberries are harvested in June which signals it's time for a Clover Club. Named after the Philadelphia gentlemen's club where it was first created in the 1800s, this is a sharp pre-Prohibition gin sour enlivened by raspberries.

### Clover Club

*2 measures gin*
*¾ measure lemon Juice*
*¾ measure sugar syrup*
*5 raspberries*
*½ measure egg white*

Add all of the ingredients to your cocktail shaker and vigorously dry-shake without ice for 10 seconds. Take the shaker apart, add cubed ice and shake again vigorously. Strain into a coupette glass and garnish with raspberries.

## 24 JUNE

The Albermarle Fizz is a long Clover Club. Sharp, fruity and refreshing, this is perfect for a long summer's evening.

### Albermarle Fizz

*2 measures gin*
*¾ measure lemon juice*
*¼ measure sugar syrup*
*¼ measure raspberry syrup*
*soda water, to top*
*lemon and raspberries, to garnish*

Add all the ingredients except the soda water to a cocktail shaker, shake vigorously and strain into a highball glass filled with cubed ice. Top with soda water and garnish with raspberries and a lemon wedge.

## 25 JUNE

*Famous Birthday: George Orwell*
Writer George Orwell was born on this day in 1901. In his book *1984*, the main character, Winston, drinks Victory Gin, a foul-sounding spirit that Orwell

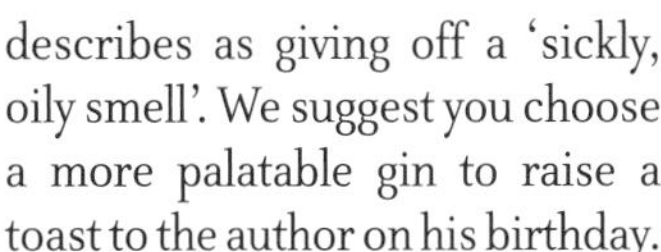

describes as giving off a 'sickly, oily smell'. We suggest you choose a more palatable gin to raise a toast to the author on his birthday.

## 26 JUNE

An extension of the ubiquitous Pimms and Lemonade by way of gin and ginger ale, this gingery deliciousness is perfect to share on a summer afternoon.

### On the Lawn

*1 measure Pimms No. 1*
*1 measure gin*
*2 measures lemonade*
*2 measures ginger ale*
*cucumber, orange and strawberries, to garnish.*

Add all of the ingredients to a highball glass filled with cubed ice, and stir. Garnish with the slices of cucumber, orange and strawberries.

## 27 JUNE

## National Pineapple Day (US)

Happy National Pineapple Day! Celebrate the tropical fruit dressed up as a pine cone in a punk wig with this ginny French Martini-Cosmopolitan dressed up as a Sidecar.

### Lady of Leisure

*1 measure gin*
*½ measure Chambord*
*½ measure Cointreau*
*¼ measure lemon juice*
*1 measure pineapple juice*
*orange, to garnish*

Add all of the ingredients to your cocktail shaker, shake vigorously and strain into a coupette glass. Garnish with an orange twist.

## 28 June

It's Wimbledon week. Hats are to horseracing as strawberries and cream are to tennis, and the strawberry/cream/tennis tradition is as old as the tournament itself. This is a frothy and luxurious strawberry fizz, with floral notes of camomile wafting around in the background like a sunstruck line umpire.

### Strawberry Fields

*2 measures gin*
*1 camomile tea bag*
*1 measure strawberry purée*
*2 tsp lemon juice*
*1 measure double cream*
*soda water, to top*
*strawberry, to garnish*

Add the gin and tea bag to a cocktail shaker and leave to infuse for 2 minutes, stirring occasionally. Remove the tea bag and add the rest of the ingredients to the shaker. Shake vigorously, strain into a wine glass full of cubed ice and top with soda water. Garnish with a strawberry.

## 29 June

We're going to go one better than strawberry, cream and gin. Ready? Strawberry. Cream. Gin. Cake.

### Strawberry & Gin Cupcakes

*Makes 12*

*75g (3oz) dried strawberries*
*6 tablespoons gin*
*125g (4oz) lightly salted butter*
*125g (4oz) caster sugar*
*finely grated zest and juice of 1 lime*
*2 eggs*
*150g (5oz) self-raising flour*
*½ teaspoon baking powder*
*150ml (¼ pint) double cream*
*12 fresh strawberries*

→

Line a 12-section cupcake tray with paper cake cases. Roughly chop the dried strawberries and put in a small bowl with the gin. Cover and leave to soak for at least 2 hours so the strawberries plump up nicely.

Drain the strawberries, reserving the gin. Put the butter, sugar, lime zest, eggs, flour and baking powder in a bowl and beat until light and creamy. Stir in the strawberries. Divide the mixture between the paper cases.

Bake in a preheated oven, 180°C (350°F), Gas Mark 4, for 20 minutes or until risen and just firm to the touch. Transfer to a wire rack to cool.

Mix the lime juice with the reserved gin. Pierce the cakes all over with a skewer and drizzle over the gin mixture.

Whip the cream until it is just beginning to hold its shape, and pipe or spoon it over the cakes. Decorate each with a whole fresh strawberry.

# 30 JUNE

*Game: Medusa*

You don't need any equipment to play this game, other than a group of friends and your drink of choice. Everyone has to sit around the table and begin each round with their eyes closed and their heads resting on the table. On the count of three, quickly lift your head and stare at another player. If the person you have chosen to stare at is looking at someone else, you're safe. If they're looking back at you, you have to shout 'Medusa!' and take a drink.

Simple, but deadly.

JULY

## 1 July

Rubies are July's birthstone so begin this sparkling month with a Ruby Fizz – a bittersweet and tangy sloe gin fizz.

### Ruby Fizz

*2 measures sloe gin*
*¾ measure lemon juice*
*¾ measure grenadine*
*1 egg white*
*soda water, to top*
*raspberries, to garnish*

Add of all the ingredients except the soda water to your cocktail shaker. Shake vigorously, strain into a highball glass full of cubed ice and top with soda. Garnish with raspberries.

## 2 July

*Tip: Pomegranate Garnish*

Jewel-like pomegranate seeds make a beautiful garnish for a summery cocktail, and their tart yet sweet flavour pairs perfectly with the botanicals in gin.

## 3 July

If at first you don't succeed... try, try a gin.

## 4 July

### Independence Day (US)

Independence Day is a day of celebration in the US, with fireworks, barbecues, carnivals and parades aplenty. Pop a sparkler in your G&T and fire up the barbecue. →

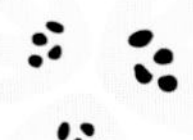

## Boozy Barbecue Sauce

*Makes 200ml (7oz)*

*2 tablespoons olive oil*
*1 small onion, finely chopped*
*1 garlic clove, crushed*
*2 teaspoons ground coriander*
*1 teaspoon ground cumin*
*¼ teaspoon ground cinnamon*
*400g (14oz) can chopped tomatoes*
*3 tablespoons maple syrup*
*2 tablespoons red wine vinegar*
*2 tablespoons gin*
*2 teaspoons hot chilli sauce*
*salt and black pepper*

Heat the oil in a saucepan and gently fry the onion, garlic and spices for 10 minutes until they are softened but not browned. Add the tomatoes, maple syrup, vinegar, gin, chilli sauce and some salt and pepper and bring to a boil. Simmer gently for 10 minutes.

Transfer to a food processor or blender and blend until smooth. This will keep in an airtight container in the refrigerator for up to 1 week.

# 5 July

# National Hawaii Day (US)

Aloha! Celebrate with this fruity highball in the style of a Tiki punch. The dryness of the gin really cuts though the tropical sweetness.

## Honolulu

*2 measures gin*
*¾ measure lemon juice*
*½ measure grenadine*
*1 measure orange juice*
*3 measures pineapple juice*
*pineapple and cocktail cherries, to garnish*

Add of all the ingredients to your cocktail shaker, shake vigorously and strain into a hurricane glass. Garnish with a pineapple wedge and a cocktail cherry.

## 6 JULY

*Tip: Freezy Does It*

Thanks to its high alcohol content, neat gin doesn't freeze. Although that sadly means you won't be enjoying a pure gin ice lolly any time soon, it does mean you can keep a bottle in the freezer ready for ice-cold cocktails whenever you please.

## 7 JULY

This is the perfect cocktail for an ice-cold gin. A spicier and more savoury alternative to the Cuban classic, the British Mojito retains a pleasant floral softness from elderflower. A summer garden in a glass. →

### British Mojito

*2 measures gin*
*¾ measure lime juice*
*½ measure elderflower cordial*
*6–8 mint leaves*
*soda, to top*
*lime and mint, to garnish*

Add of all the ingredients except the soda water to a highball glass. Fill the glass with crushed ice, and churn with a bar spoon. Add a splash of soda water, and top up with more crushed ice. Garnish with a lime wedge and a mint sprig.

## 8 JULY

*Gineral Knowledge: Beaks*

In the 17th–19th centuries, plague doctors wore strange-looking beak-like masks. Although they look scary, the purpose of these masks wasn't to frighten germs away. At the time, it was thought that the disease was spread by unclean air, so the 'beaks' were stuffed with aromatics, including juniper berries, to protect the wearer.

## 9 JULY

*Gineral Knowledge: Genever*

Genever is the traditional Dutch liquor from which gin was derived. It was initially a distillation of malt wine infused with herbs and spices, the most predominant being juniper ('genever' is the Dutch word for 'juniper'). Over time, and as production methods improved, two dominant styles emerged, those of Oude (old) Genever and Jonge (young) Genever – the differences in them referring to the cereals that went into their respective blends, as opposed to aging.

## 10 JULY

## National Piña Colada Day (US)

Yes, you read it right. Happy, happy National Piña Colada Day to you.

Pedants would insist that rum should take centre stage today but we aren't pedants. A Piña Colada is all about the coconut and pineapple and so in essence, this is a Piña Colada. Turned blue. Because why the hell not on National Piña Colada Day?

### Blue Hawaiian

*2 measures gin*
*½ measure blue curaçao*
*1 measure coconut cream*
*3 measures pineapple juice*
*pineapple and cocktail cherry, to garnish*

Add of all the ingredients to a food processor or blender and blend with a handful of cubed ice. Pour into a hurricane glass and garnish with a pineapple wedge and a cocktail cherry.

## 11 JULY

*Gineral Knowledge: Blue Curaçao*
Blue curaçao is simply orange curaçao, which is distilled to have no colour, turned blue with flavourless blue food colouring. It may have lost its exotic or mysterious edge but it's a wonderfully silly addition to just about anything liquid.

## 12 JULY

A generous splash of gin makes this zesty coconut cake extra-special.

### Lime, Gin & Coconut Drizzle Cake

*Serves 8*

*200g (7oz) unsalted butter, softened*
*200g (7oz) caster sugar*
*finely grated zest and juice of 2 limes*
*3 eggs, lightly beaten*
*200g (7oz) self-raising flour, sifted*
*50g (2oz) desiccated coconut*

*For the topping*
*4 tablespoons caster sugar*
*2 tablespoons gin*
*2 tablespoons desiccated or shredded coconut*
*finely pared strands of lemon zest*

Grease a 20cm (8in) round springform cake tin and line the base with nonstick baking parchment.
Beat the eggs, sugar and lime zest together in a large bowl until pale and fluffy. Beat in the eggs a little at a time, adding 1 tablespoon of the flour if the mixture starts to curdle, then fold in the flour and coconut with a large metal spoon.
Spoon into the prepared tin and bake in a preheated oven, 180°C (350°F), Gas Mark 4, for 35–40 minutes until risen and golden and shrinking from the tin.
Leave to cool in the tin for 5 minutes. While the cake is still warm, mix the sugar with the lime juice and gin and spoon over the cake. Sprinkle over the coconut and lime zest strands and leave to cool completely.

## 13 JULY

*Game: Two Truths and a Lie*

Next time you're having trouble deciding whose turn it is to go to the bar, have a quick round of Two Truths and a Lie. One person has to say three things about themselves – two must be true, and one must be a lie. The idea is to make it as tricky as possible for the other players to work out. The other players have to figure out which of their statements is false – and whoever gets it wrong has to get the next round in. This is also a good one to play at parties as an ice-breaker, as it never fails to get the conversation flowing.

## 14 JULY

*Famous Birthday: Phoebe Waller-Bridge*

The multi-talented Phoebe Waller-Bridge was born on this day in 1985. Celebrate the birth of the creator of *Fleabag* with a can of ready-mixed gin and tonic like the one she shared with the Priest in season two.

## 15 JULY

Summer is heating up and it's time to go bananas with the tropical fruit. Underneath its prickly lizard skin, the lychee is a juicy jewel with a delicate, floral flavour.

### Lychee Martini

*1½ measures gin*
*1 measure lychee liqueur*
*½ measure lychee syrup (from the tin)*
*¾ measure lemon juice*
*lychees (tinned), to garnish*

Add of all the ingredients to your cocktail shaker, shake vigorously and double strain into a chilled martini glass. Garnish with lychees and a little wiggle.

## 16 July

For something longer, try this bittersweet highball cooler.

### Lychee & Campari Cooler

*1½ measures gin*
*½ measure Campari*
*½ measure lemon juice*
*¾ measure lychee syrup (from the tin)*
*soda to top*
*orange and lychees, to garnish*

Add all of the ingredients except the soda water to a highball glass, stirring in cubed ice as you go. Top with soda, and garnish with an orange wedge and lychees.

## 17 July

*Craft: Gin Glass Charms*

There is nothing more saddening than realizing that someone else has been mistakenly taking swigs of your drink all evening. To prevent confusion at your next party, make some simple charms that you and your guests can attach to your glasses to help you remember whose is whose.

All you need is some modelling wire and some coloured glass or plastic beads in a variety of colours. Simply thread a bead onto a piece of wire, then twist the ends. If you're drinking out of stemmed glasses, the wire can be wrapped around the stem. If not, fashion it into a shape a bit like a dangly earring and hang it over the rim of your glass. Just make sure each charm uses a different colour bead – and remember which colour is yours!

## 18 July

Nothing says summer like fresh mint. This is somewhere between a Mojito and a Julep.

### Gin Cup

*2 measures gin*
*¾ measure lemon juice*
*½ measure sugar syrup*
*3 mint sprigs, plus extra to garnish*

Muddle the mint and sugar syrup in an old fashioned glass. Fill the glass with crushed ice, add the gin and lemon and churn vigorously until a frost begins to form on the glass. Garnish with mint sprigs.

## 19 July

Beat the summer heat with these refreshing grown-up lollies.

### Minty G&T Lollies

*Makes 10*

*450ml (¾ pint) Indian tonic water*
*100ml (3½fl oz) elderflower cordial*
*75ml (3fl oz) gin*
*juice of 1 lime*
*20 small mint leaves*

In a jug, mix the tonic water, elderflower cordial, lime juice and gin.
Pour into 10 x 90ml (3¼fl oz) ice lolly moulds and add 2 mint leaves to each mould. Insert lolly sticks and freeze until solid, preferably overnight.

## 20 JULY

*Gineral Knowledge: Vapour Infusion*

Vapour infusion simply means that the botanicals are held in baskets, usually copper, and suspended above the grain spirit during the distillation process, as opposed to being submerged within it. As a result, the vapours of the spirit pass through the baskets, infusing the condensed distillate with the flavours of the botanicals. Vapour infusion will often lead to a softer, more complex finished product.

## 21 JULY

*Famous Birthday: Ernest Hemingway*

Writer and all-round good egg Ernest Hemingway was born on this day in 1899. Although his fondness for daiquiris is well-known, he is also said to have enjoyed a concoction of gin and coconut water. The drink makes an appearance in his novel *Islands in the Stream*, where it is called a Green Isaac Special: 'a tall, cold drink made of gin, lime juice, green coconut water and chipped ice, with just enough Angostura bitters to give it a rusty rose colour'.

## 22 JULY

An enticing coconut daiquiri, with hints of tropical pineapple and refreshing mint. Apparently divised in the bath by London bartender of note Liam Cotter at Highwater, London in 2015.

### Surface To Air

*1 measure coconut rum*
*1 measure gin*
*¾ measure lime juice*
*½ measure fresh pineapple juice*
*½ measure sugar syrup*
*8 mint leaves*

Add of all the ingredients to your cocktail shaker, shake vigorously and double strain into a chilled coupette glass. No garnish.

## 23 JULY

*Famous Birthday: Raymond Chandler*

The recipe for the sweet, sharp and strong Gimlet has evolved with time, and varies from source to source. According to Raymond Chandler 'A real Gimlet is half gin and half Rose's lime juice and nothing else', while others call for fresh lime and a touch of sugar syrup. Birthday Rules dictate that we can't argue with Chandler, but here's a compromise:

### Gimlet

*2½ measures gin*
*½ measure lime cordial*
*½ measure lime juice*
*lime, to garnish*

Add of all the ingredients to your cocktail shaker, shake vigorously and strain into a chilled coupette glass. Garnish with a lime twist.

## 24 JULY

## National Tequila Day (US)

Rising to fame in the 1980s and still enormously popular today, the Long Island Iced Tea takes almost all of the most well-known light spirits and sweetens them with cola.

### Long Island Ice Tea

*½ measure vodka*
*½ measure gin*
*½ measure white rum*
*½ measure tequila*
*½ measure triple sec*
*¾ measure lemon juice*
*½ measure sugar syrup*
*cola, to top*
*lemon, to garnish*

Add of all the ingredients except the cola to your cocktail shaker, shake and strain into a hurricane glass filled with cubed ice and top with cola. Garnish with a wedge of lemon.

## 25 July

*Game: Tongue Twister*

Tongue twisters are tricky at the best of times, but after a glass or two they can get even more challenging. Next time you're sharing cocktails with friends, give this one a go, saying it over and over as fast as you can:

*Juicy jazzy juniper is just in genuine gin.*

## 26 July

The warmer and drier summer months are the best for growing and harvesting basil. Basil is a member of the mint family and just like its fragrant and mintier cousin, it brings a wonderful waft of herby notes to a drink. Use it as a garnish for a G&T or try a Rhubarb and Strawberry Daisy – halfway between a martini and a spritz, this is a real celebration drink with perfectly balanced summer flavours. →

### Rhubarb & Strawberry Daisy

*1½ measures gin*
*¾ measure rhubarb liqueur*
*½ measure lemon juice*
*2 strawberries*
*6 basil leaves*
*Prosecco, to top*

Quickly muddle the strawberries and five basil leaves in the base of your cocktail shaker, add the gin, rhubarb liqueur and lemon juice and shake vigorously. Double strain into a martini glass, top with Prosecco and garnish with the remaining basil leaf.

## 27 JULY

A ginny, herby and fruity Mojito-style summer cooler. Delicious.

### Strawberry & Basil Smash

*2 measures gin*
*½ measure lemon juice*
*¼ measure sugar syrup*
*3 stawberries*
*6 basil leaves*
*soda, to top*
*strawberry and basil, to garnish*

Half-fill a highall glass with crushed ice. Add of all the ingredients and churn vigorously. Top with more crushed ice and a splash of soda water, and garnish with a half a strawberry and a basil leaf.

## 28 JULY

*Tip: Chill Your Glasses*

Sometimes the simplest things can make a huge difference. Next time you plan to mix up a G&T, pop your glasses in the freezer for about an hour beforehand. The ice-cold glasses will make your drinks extra refreshing.

## 29 JULY

*Gineral Knowledge: Vacuum Distillation*

Vacuum distillation, or cold distillation, is a process where botanical infusion takes place in a vacuum. The advantage here is that it means the distiller is not bound to alcohol's, (or more specifically, ethanol's) boiling point – and they are able to distill at a lower temperature which allows different aspects of certain botanicals to reveal themselves in ways not previously seen.

## 30 JULY
# International Day of Friendship

Get your best buds together and enjoy a ginny, summery feast. This salad works wonderfully as a shareable small plate, or pairs perfectly with pork or lamb.

## Fennel & Radish Salad with Gin Dressing

*Serves 4*

*2 fennel bulbs, about 650g (1lb 5oz) in total*
*300g (10oz) radishes, trimmed*
*2 tablespoons roughly chopped parsley*

*For the gin dressing*
*3 tablespoons lemon juice*
*1 tablespoon gin*
*2 tablespoons extra virgin olive oil*
*salt and black pepper*

Slice the fennel and radishes as thinly as possible on a mandolin or with a knife. Toss together in a large bowl with the parsley. →

Make the dressing by whisking together the lemon juice, gin and oil. Season to taste with salt and pepper.
Pour the dressing over the salad and toss gently to mix.

## 31 JULY

See out the last evening of July in sultry summer style with a Lychee Negroni. All of the best bits of the classic Negroni are present, but are softened and slightly sweetened by bianco vermouth and lychee.

## Lychee Negroni

*¾ measure gin*
*1½ measures bianco vermouth*
*½ measure Campari*
*1 measure lychee juice*
*cucumber, to garnish*

Build all the ingredients in a rocks glass full of cubed ice, stir briefly and garnish with a slice of cucumber.

# AUGUST

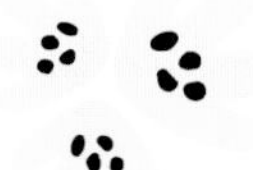

## 1 AUGUST

*Gineral Knowledge: Dutch Courage*

These days, we tend to think of 'Dutch courage' as taking a fortifying gulp of your drink before bravely asking someone for their number, but where does the phrase come from? It's thought to have its origins in the Anglo-Dutch Wars of the mid-1600s, when genever (a Dutch liquor made of juniper and sometimes referred to as 'Dutch gin') was apparently drunk before battle in an effort to combat nerves.

## 2 AUGUST

*Tip: Cucumber Twist*

The cool, and fresh flavour of cucumber is the perfect addition to your gin and tonic on a hot summer's day. You could just pop a couple of slices into your tumbler, but for extra style, use a vegetable peeler to slice long, green ribbons of cucumber to curl around the inside of your glass.

## 3 AUGUST

A mojito alternative for gin lovers, the cucumber brings a welcome freshness to this pleasant summer sipper.

### Cucumber Cooler

*2 measures gin*
*½ measure sugar syrup*
*½ measure lemon juice*
*5 pieces cucumber*
*6 mint leaves*
*soda water, to top*
*cucumber and mint, to garnish*

Add all of the ingredients except the soda water to a highball glass and muddle. Fill the glass with crushed ice and churn. Top with soda water. Garnish with slices of cucumber and a mint sprig.

## 4 AUGUST

*Famous Birthday: Queen Elizabeth The Queen Mother*
'I think that I will take two small bottles of Dubonnet and gin with me this morning, in case it is needed' once noted Elizabeth Bowes-Lyons, before taking a trip. An excellent idea.

### Queen Mother Cocktail

*2 measures Dubonnet*
*1 measure gin*
*lemon, to garnish*

Add both ingredients to an old fashioned glass filled with cubed ice, stir briefly and garnish with a slice of lemon.

## 5 AUGUST

### World Oyster Day

Proving once again that there really is a day for everything, and that that everything can always be paired with gin, behold...the Oyster Shot. With a quick wallop of Bloody Mary goodness, this would make for a decadent (if hit-and-miss) hangover cure, but it really comes into its own on World Oyster Day.

### Oyster Shot

*¾ measure gin*
*¾ measure tomato juice*
*4 drops Tabasco sauce*
*3 dashes Worcestershire sauce*
*pinch celery salt*
*pinch black pepper*
*1 fresh oyster*

Add all the ingredients except the oyster to your cocktail shaker, shake vigorously and double strain into a rocks glass. Drop in the oyster, close your eyes and knock it back.

# 6 AUGUST

Lest we forgot mussels in the whirl and spin of Oyster Day...

## Spicy Gin-Steamed Mussels

*Serves 4*

*1 tablespoon groundnut oil*
*2 shallots, thinly sliced*
*1 red chilli, deseeded and finely sliced*
*2.5cm (1in) piece of fresh root ginger, peeled and finely chopped*
*1 garlic clove, finely sliced*
*3 tablespoons gin*
*350ml (12fl oz) fish or vegetable stock*
*1 small preserved lemon, finely chopped*
*1.5kg (3lb) mussels, scrubbed and debearded*
*1 small bunch of coriander, roughly chopped*
*salt and black pepper*

→

Heat the oil in a large, heavy-based saucepan over medium–low heat, then stir in the shallots, chilli, ginger and garlic and cook gently for 7–8 minutes or until softened, stirring occasionally. Add the gin and simmer to evaporate, then add the stock and preserved lemon and bring to boiling point.

Tip in the mussels, discarding any that won't close. Season with salt and pepper, then stir the mussels to coat in the shallot mix. Cover the pan with a tight-fitting lid and steam gently, shaking the pan occasionally, for 4–5 minutes. Part way through cooking, stir the mussels thoroughly, lifting the ones from the bottom to the top and replace the lid.

Once the mussels are cooked, heap into bowls, discarding any that remain closed, scatter over the coriander and serve immediately.

## 7 AUGUST

*Game: Who Am I?*

A fun ice-breaker game for your next cocktail party. Get into pairs and give each person a sticky note and a pen. Without their partner seeing the name, each person should write the name of a famous person (real or fictitious, living or dead) and stick it to their partner's forehead. Once everyone has a name tag, you can all move around the room, asking other people questions in an effort to figure out who you are. The first person to guess correctly gets to choose the next cocktail.

## 8 AUGUST

*Gineral Knowledge: Old Tom Gin*

Hailing from 18th century London, many a very silly story surrounds Old Tom Gin's true beginnings, one of them even involving an unfortunate and clumsy cat (look it up...). But in essence, its style could be described as a more botanical-heavy, and slightly sweeter version of the London Dry Gin that we drink today.

## 9 AUGUST

The second Sunday of August marks National Melon Day in Turkmenistan. And why not? Established in 1994, it is a public holiday devoted to the muskmelon – a variety of melon that includes the honeydew and cantaloupe melons that might be more familiar to us than a true, musky muskmelon.

Raise a toast with this crisply fruited gin frappé, topped with sparkling wine and with a welcome spike of anise. In many respects, the perfect drink. ➔

## Honeydew

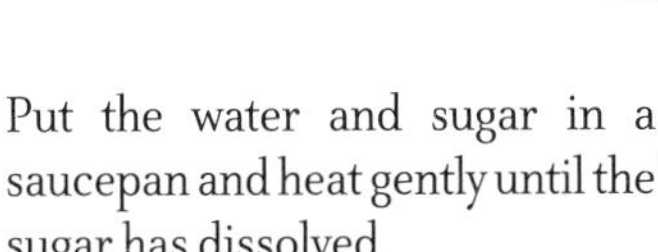

*1 measure gin*
*½ measure lemon juice*
*½ measure sugar syrup*
*2 drops absinthe (or Pernod)*
*5 cubes honeydew melon*
*Prosecco, to top*
*lemon and rosemary, to garnish*

Add all of the ingredients except the Prosecco to a blender or food processor and blend with 5 cubes of ice. Pour into a chilled wine glass, top with Champagne and garnish with a lemon twist and sprig of rosemary.

# 10 AUGUST

Easy to make, this icy sweet treat is perfect to enjoy on a hot day.

## Watermelon & Gin Granita

*Serves 6*

*150g (5oz) caster sugar*
*150ml (¼ pint) water*
*2kg (4lb) watermelon*
*2 tablespoons lemon juice*
*4 tablespoons gin*

➜

Put the water and sugar in a saucepan and heat gently until the sugar has dissolved.

Slice the watermelon into wedges, cut away the skin and remove the pips. Blend the flesh in a food processor or blender until smooth, or rub through a sieve.

Strain the watermelon purée into a freezer container and stir in the sugar mixture, lemon juice and gin. Freeze for 3–4 hours until it is turning mushy. Mash with a fork and refreeze for 2–3 hours until it reaches the mushy stage again. Repeat the process once or twice more until the granita is evenly mushy. This can be frozen until required.

Fork through the granita to break up the ice and pile into glasses to serve.

## 11 AUGUST

*Famous Birthday: Enid Blyton*
Children's book writer Enid Blyton was born on this day in 1897. To mark the day, make like the Famous Five and have a picnic. Be sure to serve your gin with lashings of ginger beer.

## 12 AUGUST

For a real treat of a summer spritz, and a perfect serve to scale up into a jug for picnics in the garden, try a Cupid's Spritz. Gin and edible flowers AND chocolate liqueur.

### Cupid's Spritz

*1 measure gin*
*1 measure rosé vermouth*
*½ measure white chocolate liqueur*
*tonic, to top*
*orange and edible flowers, to garnish*

Add all of the ingredients to a large wine glass full of cubed ice, stir briefly and garnish with slices of orange and edible flowers.

## 13 AUGUST

*Gineral Knowledge: Spritz*
The concept of the 'spritz' began in Austrian-occupied Italy in the 1800s, when the Habsburg soldiers found the local wine in Venato too varied, complex and strong for their tastes, and so diluted it with soda water. Over time the Italians adopted the convention, and improved the idea by subtly adding their own bitter vermouths and spirits; creating complex, refreshing and low alcohol drinks that are now adored the world over.

## 14 AUGUST

*Tip: Get Creative*

As a general rule of thumb, if it looks pretty or smells pretty, it'll go pretty well with a G&T.

Try basil, lemon thyme, lemon verbena leaf, mint, rosemary, jasmine flowers, pansies, pink peppercorns and kumquats.

## 15 AUGUST

On this day in 1959, the first Woodstock music festival opened. Although nothing can come close to what was probably the very most important moment in modern music, this cocktail is trying its best. An enlivened 'gin and orange', it's pleasantly dry out of the rain with hippie floral notes. →

### Woodstock

*1½ measures gin*
*1 measure dry vermouth*
*½ measure Cointreau*
*½ measure lemon juice*
*2 tbsp sugar syrup*
*4 measures orange juice*
*orange, to garnish*

Add all of the ingredients to your cocktail shaker, shake vigorously and strain into a highball glass. Garnish with slices of orange.

## 16 AUGUST

*Know Your Glassware: Rocks Glass*

The rocks glass, also known as the old fashioned glass or lowball, is a short, wide tumbler. It's often used for serving spirits neat over ice, or for cocktails like the eponymous Old Fashioned that require ingredients to be muddled in the glass. These short, stocky glasses are also perfect for a Negroni.

## 17 AUGUST

It's time to put your new-found knowledge of the rocks glass to good use. Try this: gin's answer to the Caipiroska, though closer to a gin sour on the rocks in style.

### Ginpiroska

*2 measures gin*
*1 measure lime juice*
*¾ measure sugar syrup*
*lime, to garnish*

Fill a rocks glass with crushed ice, add all the ingredients and churn vigorously. Top with more crushed ice and garnish with a lime wedge.

## 18 AUGUST

*Gineral Knowledge: BOOM!*
In the 1800s, British naval officers received a ration of gin as part of their pay. Legend has it that a common test to make sure it hadn't been watered down was to pour a little of the gin on to some gunpowder and check to make sure it would still catch fire.

## 19 AUGUST

*Famous Birthday: Ogden Nash*
American poet Ogden Nash was born on this day in 1902. Enjoy a martini in his honour, while reciting the following verse from his poem *A Drink With Something In It*:
'There is something about a martini,/Ere the dining and dancing begin/And to tell you the truth it's not the vermouth –/I think that perhaps it's the gin.'

## 20 AUGUST

Ogden Nash might just have been on to something, so here's a martini that does away with the vermouth entirely and is probably the fanciest way to drink gin and orange to boot…

### Opal Martini

*2 measures gin*
*¾ measure Cointreau*
*2 measures orange juice*
*2 dashes sugar syrup*
*orange twist, to garnish*

Add all of the ingredients to your cocktail shaker, shake vigorously and strain into a chilled coupette. Garnish with an orange twist.

## 21 AUGUST

Today's drink is a gin and cherry julep, and a marvellous alternative to the bourbon-based original. Perfect on a hot summer's day.

### Cherry Julep

*¾ measure gin*
*¾ measure sloe gin*
*¾ measure cherry brandy*
*¾ measure lemon juice*
*1 tsp sugar syrup*
*1 tsp grenadine*
*lemon and mint, to garnish*

Fill a highball glass with crushed ice, add all the ingredients and churn vigorously. Top with more crushed ice and garnish with a wedge of lemon and a mint sprig.

## 22 AUGUST

*Famous Birthday: Dorothy Parker*
Poet, writer, satirist and critic, and all-round legend Dorothy Parker was only persuaded to add gin to her list of favourite tipples when it was mixed in a martini. To celebrate her birthday we'll share one of our favourites of her many witty wisecracks on the subject: 'I like to have a martini, two at the very most. After three I'm under the table, after four, I'm under my host.'

## 23 AUGUST

Pink and fluffy, a crowd pleasing modern classic: the French Martini is just silly enough to be taken seriously. Dorothy Parker would have had a lot to say about this one. ➔

### French Martini

*1½ measures gin*
*1 measure Chambord*
*2 measures pineapple juice*
*raspberries, to garnish*

Add all of the ingredients to your cocktail shaker, shake vigorously and strain into a chilled coupette glass. Garnish with raspberries.

## 24 AUGUST

*Game: Drink Murder*
We all remember playing Wink Murder (or Blink Murder, for those of us who couldn't wink) at birthday parties. This is a slightly more grown-up version. One player is chosen to be the Detective and sent out of the room. The other players must choose among themselves who the Murderer will be. When the Detective returns, the Murderer can begin their killing spree – but instead of winking (or blinking) at their victims, they must make eye contact with them while drinking.

If the Murderer looks at you while taking a sneaky sip of their drink, you have to 'die' – preferably, as theatrically as possible. Other players can make it even harder for the Detective by continuing to enjoy their own drinks as normal. The Detective has to figure out who the Murderer is before the guests all 'die' – or before the Murderer's glass is empty.

## 25 AUGUST

Packed with nutrients and among the prettiest fruits ever to fall into a fruit salad, the kiwifruit – or Chinese gooseberry – brings a wonderful tartness and sweetness to a cocktail.

A citrussy, emerald-green gin Fix, the Kiwi Smash is an exotic and summery alternative to the Ginpiroska. Smashing. →

### Kiwi Smash

*2 measures gin*
*¾ measure lime juice*
*½ measure sugar syrup*
*1 kiwifruit, peeled and cubed*
*lime, to garnish*

Drop the kiwifruit into a rocks glass, and muddle with a spoon. Add the remaining ingredients, fill the glass with crushed ice and churn. Top with more crushed ice and garnish with a lime wedge.

## 26 AUGUST

A kiwi-green, refreshing and fruity slushie.

### Green Bay Colada

*2 measures gin*
*½ measure lime juice*
*1 measure agave syrup*
*½ kiwifruit, peeled*
*5 cubes cantaloupe melon*
*mint, to garnish*

Add all of the ingredients, and 7 cubes of ice, to a blender or food processer and blend until smooth. Pour into a rocks glass and garnish with a sprig of mint.

## 27 AUGUST

*Gineral Knowledge: Juniper Berries*
Forget everything you think you know – juniper berries aren't actually berries at all. They are in fact the seed cones of the female juniper plant. Essentially, they're tasty pinecones. YUM.

## 28 AUGUST

*Game: I'm Going to the Bar and I'm Getting...*
This is a fun memory game that seems easy at first, but quickly gets devilishly tricky. The first person begins by saying: 'I'm going to the bar and I'm getting a gin and tonic' (of course). The second person has to repeat this, but add their own drink to the order, for example: 'I'm going to the bar and I'm getting a gin and tonic and a Tom Collins'. You continue on around the table, with the drinks list growing longer and longer. The first person to forget has to get the next round in (although you should probably write the order down for them, as they've already shown they can't be trusted to remember).

## 29 AUGUST

*Famous Birthday:*
*Harry Craddock*
Harry Craddock (1876 – 1963) was an English Bartender of global fame, garnered most notably from his tenure as Head Bartender of the American Bar of the Savoy Hotel London in the 1920s and 30s. When Prohibition laws hit in the US, some of the country's best bartenders jumped ship and headed to the UK. London in particular benefited from an influx of creative cocktail experts, including the legendary Harry Craddock. Although born in the UK, he had been living and working in New York for decades. When Prohibition began, he came back to London. A forefather of modern bartending, dozens of his recipes are still imbibed to this day. In 1930 he published *The Savoy Cocktail Book*, arguably the most important cocktail book of the 20th century.

## 30 AUGUST

A classic from *The Savoy Cocktail Book* by Harry Craddock, bright and elegant.

### Maiden's Blush

*1½ measures gin*
*1 measure orange curaçao*
*½ measure lemon juice*
*2 tsp grenadine*
*2 tsp sugar syrup*
*lemon, to garnish*

Add all of the ingredients to your cocktail shaker, shake vigorously and strain into a chilled coupette. Garnish with a lemon twist.

## 31 AUGUST

On this day in 1967, poet Philip Larkin completed his poem *Sympathy in White Major*, which included the lines:
'When I drop four cubes of ice
Chimingly in a glass, and add
Three goes of gin, a lemon slice...'

# SEPTEMBER

## 1 SEPTEMBER

### Blackberry Gin

September heralds the return of blackberries to the hedgerows. Tart and bursting with flavour, blackberries are a wonderful fruit to infuse with gin. Simply wash about 300g (10oz) blackberries and place them in a sterilized jar along with 100g (3oz) sugar. Pour in 500ml (17fl oz) of gin, seal the lid, give the jar a shake and place it somewhere cool and dark for a week. Give the jar a shake every other day to help the sugar dissolve. After a week, strain the liquid through a muslin or very fine sieve, bottle it and drink it within a month.

## 2 SEPTEMBER

Created by the late, great Dick Bradsell in the 1980s, this gin sour flavoured with crème de mure is a true modern classic. Sharp, fruity and boozy. Seasonal and sensational.

### Bramble

*2 measures gin*
*1 measure lemon juice*
*½ measure sugar syrup*
*½ measure crème de mure*
*lemon and blackberries, to garnish*

Fill an old fashioned glass with crushed ice, packing it in tightly. Add the gin, lemon juice and sugar syrup and stir briefly. Slowly drizzle over the crème de mure, so that it creates a 'bleeding' effect down through the drink. Top with more crushed ice and garnish with blackberries and a lemon wedge.

## 3 SEPTEMBER

*Gineral Knowledge: The Gin Acts*
When the Gin Acts of the 1700s were brought in to restrict the consumption of gin in the UK, drinkers across the country were so distraught that they are said to have held mock funerals mourning the passing of 'Madam Geneva', (a pun on genever). A 1736 engraving entitled *The Funeral Procession of Madam Geneva* shows a crowd of mourners and a coffin topped with a glass, jug and barrel.

## 4 SEPTEMBER

Sapphire being the birthstone of September is perhaps the only excuse one needs to enjoy a Sapphire Martini. A gin martini, sweetened with orange-flavoured blue stuff. Stir this one well, as the correct amount of dilution is the key to cutting through the sweetness of the curaçao. →

### Sapphire Martini

*2 measures gin*
*½ measure blue curaçao*
*cocktail cherry, to decorate*

Add all of the ingredients to a cocktail shaker or mixing glass, and fill with cubed ice. Stir for 30 seconds, and strain into a chilled martini glass. Garnish with a cocktail cherry.

## 5 SEPTEMBER

*Game: Pictionary & Tonic*
Give every player five slips of paper and ask them to write a different item on each. You can leave it random, or you can suggest categories (e.g. animals, objects, actions, etc.). Once everybody has written down five

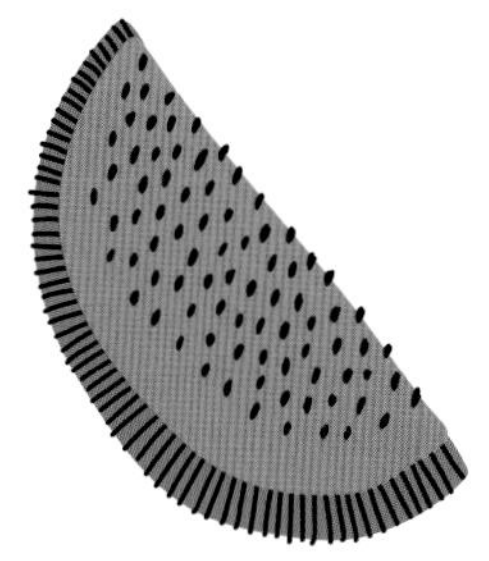

ideas, put all the pieces of paper in a hat or a bowl and mix them together. (If you prefer, you can use a random word generator online.) Divide up into teams. The first player must pick a piece of paper from the bowl and begin to draw it so that their teammates can guess what it is. The person drawing isn't allowed to speak. Someone from the other team has to time how long it takes the artist's teammates to correctly guess what they're drawing. After their turn, the artist has to take a sip of their drink for every 30 seconds it took their teammates to guess. If nobody guesses within 5 minutes, the artist must complete a forfeit (we suggest they get the next round in).

# 6 SEPTEMBER

Autumnal in feel, this is a deftly balanced gin highball with the faintest waft of Campari cutting through the rich sweetness of hedgerow fruit.

## Hedgerow Collins

*1½ measures gin*
*½ measure crème de mure*
*1 tsp Campari*
*¾ measure lemon juice*
*½ measure sugar syrup*
*soda water, to top*
*lemon and blackberry, to garnish*

Add all of the ingredients except the soda water to a highball glass filled with cubed ice. Stir gently, top with soda and garnish with a lemon wedge and a blackberry.

## 7 SEPTEMBER

Listen to *Love is Like a Bottle of Gin* by The Magnetic Fields from their 1999 album '69 Love Songs'.

## 8 SEPTEMBER

*Know Your Glassware:*
*Martini Glass*
Perhaps the most iconic cocktail glass there is, the striking silhouette and elegant lines of the martini glass make it a firm favourite that never fails to add a touch of class to proceedings. This is best suited to short cocktails that aren't served over ice, such as (of course) the martini. The wide shape allows the aromas of your drink to rise up to your nose, so it's the perfect vessel for a botanical cocktail.

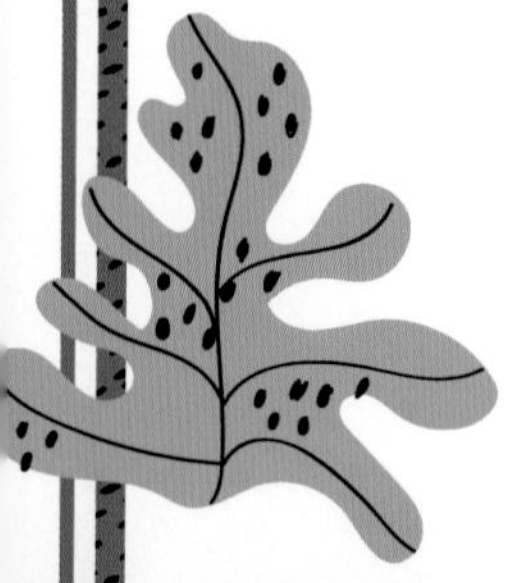

## 9 SEPTEMBER

Created in the early 1900s by Luigi Naintre at the Embassy Club, London, the Luigi is sweet, sharp and just a tiny bit floral all at once.

### Luigi

*2 measures gin*
*1 measure dry vermouth*
*½ measure Cointreau*
*1 measure grenadine*
*1 measure orange juice*
*blood orange, to garnish*

Add all of the ingredients to a cocktail shaker or mixing glass, and fill with cubed ice. Stir for 30 seconds, and strain into a chilled martini glass. Garnish with a twist of blood orange.

## 10 SEPTEMBER

*Craft: Drinkable You*
Celebrate your gin-dividuality by creating your own cocktail and naming it after yourself. Think about different elements you love from existing cocktails

and find ways to combine them, or try pairing some of your favourite flavours and garnishes. Sometimes it's the unexpected combinations that make the best cocktails, so don't be afraid to experiment.

## 11 SEPTEMBER

In the spirit of experimentation, how about using lavender flowers for a garnish on this sensational, floral and fruity gin sour?

### Kashmir

*1¾ measures gin*
*¾ measure bianco vermouth*
*¾ measure lemon juice*
*¾ measure raspberry syrup*
*1 egg white*
*lavender flowers, to garnish*

Add all of the ingredients to your cocktail shaker and dry-shake for 10 seconds. Take the shaker apart, add ice, and shake again vigorously. Strain into a coupette glass and garnish with a sprig of lavender.

## 12 SEPTEMBER

*Gineral Knowledge: International Style Gin*

The past 20-odd years have witnessed great changes in the gin world, with independent craft distillers (empowered by our collective appetite for all things gin) playing around with the traditional make-up of previously sacred recipes. Also, up until very recently, gin had retained a sort of mystical, semi-protected status of being a quintessentially 'British' drink, but this idea is fading rapidly as new distilleries pop up all over the world.

Gins are now being made in over 50 countries, and recipes are rapidly evolving using state-of-the-art distilling techniques and incorporating dozens of unique combinations of botanicals.

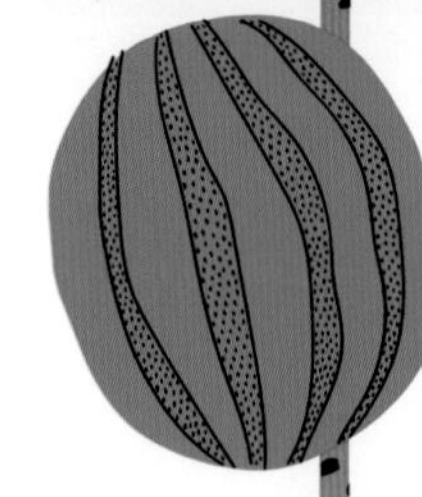

## 13 SEPTEMBER

*Famous Birthday: Roald Dahl*

The author of many much-loved children's books including *James and the Giant Peach* and *The BFG* was born on this day in 1916. In *Charlie and the Chocolate Factory*, the group of visitors being shown around by Willy Wonka pass a door marked with the words 'BUTTERSCOTCH AND BUTTERGIN', delicious concoctions which, Mr Wonka explains, 'the Oompa-Loompas all adore [...] It makes them tiddly.' Why not mark the occasion with a glass of your own marvellous medicine?

## 14 SEPTEMBER

*Tip: Season to Taste*

Black pepper pairs remarkably well with gin as it brings out the flavour of the juniper. Just finish your drink with a quick grind or two of black pepper and enjoy a whole new take on a G&T. Add a couple of sliced strawberries for a real treat.

## 15 SEPTEMBER

It isn't all about black pepper. Pink peppercorns give a wonderful spicy and citrussy heat to this tropical bellini.

### Nehru

*1 measure gin*
*4 slices mango*
*5 pink peppercorns*
*Prosecco, to top*

Add the gin, mango and the peppercorns to a blender or food processor and blend until smooth. Strain into a Champagne flute and top with chilled Prosecco.

# 16 SEPTEMBER

Spreadable gin for breakfast? Oh yes please.

## Blueberry, Apple & Gin Jam

*Makes about 3 small jars*

*1kg (2lb) blueberries*
*3 medium green apples, about 450g (14½oz), peeled, cored and finely chopped*
*2 tablespoons lemon juice*
*875g (1¾lb) granulated sugar*
*3–6 tablespoons gin*

Put the blueberries, apples and lemon juice in a large saucepan. Bring to the boil, reduce the heat and simmer, uncovered, for about 15 minutes or until the blueberries are soft.

Add the sugar and stir over a high heat, without boiling, until the sugar dissolves. Bring to the boil and boil, uncovered, for about 20 minutes. To test if the jam is ready, chill a saucer in the freezer, then drop a blob of jam onto it and let it cool. → Push the jam with your finger; the skin will wrinkle if it's ready. If not, boil for a further 5 minutes and test again.

Half-fill new, sterilized jars with the hot jam, then add 1 or 2 tablespoons of gin, to taste, to each and stir in, then top up with more jam. Stir carefully once more then seal the jars immediately.

# 17 SEPTEMBER

*Famous Birthday:*
*Sir Francis Chichester*

Businessman, aviator and sailor Sir Francis Chichester was born on this day in 1901. In 1966–67, he became the first person to sail single-handedly around the world by the clipper route. He put his success down to enjoying a daily glass of pink gin cocktail throughout the voyage, and is said to have declared: 'Any damn fool can navigate the world sober. It takes a really good sailor to do it drunk.'

## 18 September

*Gineral Knowledge: Ginspiration*

It will come as no surprise that the books we read and films we watch have a big impact on our drinking habits. British supermarket Waitrose reported a 23% increase in sales of gin after the release of Baz Luhrman's film adaptation of *The Great Gatsby*, with shoppers keen to recreate Jay Gatsby's glitzy cocktail parties at home.

## 19 September

### International Talk Like a Pirate Day

'Arrrr mateys! Yo ho ho and a bottle of... gin.'

## 20 September

Florida was literally a treasure trove for pirates in the 16th century. Spain used the Gulf Coast to harbour its fleets before they sailed back to Europe – easy pickings for the pirates hiding out in the many inlets and bays of the Florida Keys. Fit for even the scurviest of coves, channel your inner pirate-with-a-penchant-for-pie with this ginny twist on a classic no-bake key lime pie.

### Tipsy Key Lime Pie

*Serves 6–8*

*200g (7oz) digestive or ginger biscuits*
*100g (3½ oz) unsalted butter, melted*

*For the filling*
*juice and zest of 4 limes*
*3 tablespoons gin*
*400g (14oz) can sweetened condensed milk*
*300ml (½ pint) double cream*

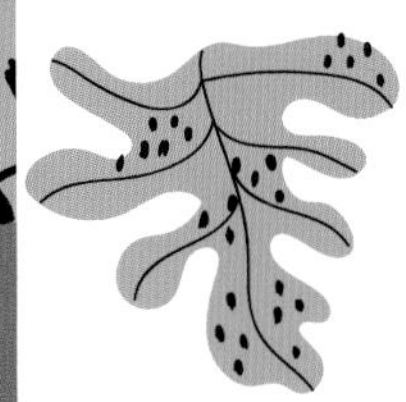

Crush the biscuits to fine crumbs by blitzing in a food processor or placing in a large plastic bag, sealing the top and crushing with a rolling pin.

Mix the biscuit crumbs with the melted butter, then press into a 23cm (9in) springform tin, lining the bottom and a little way up the sides. Chill for 10–15 minutes.

To make the filling, add all of the ingredients together in a large bowl and beat with an electric whisk until thick and creamy. Pour into the biscuit-lined tin and chill for 30 minutes or until set.

## 21 SEPTEMBER
## Sunshine State

*1 measure gin*
*½ measure elderflower liqueur*
*2 tsp lemon juice*
*1 measure apple juice*
*6 mint leaves*
*Prosecco, to top*
*strawberry, to garnish*

Squeeze the mint leaves in your hand to express the oils, then drop them into a highball glass. Add the gin, elderflower liqueur, lemon juice and apple juice, fill with cubed ice and stir well. Top with chilled Prosecco. Stir again briefly and garnish with slices of strawberry.

## 22 SEPTEMBER

*Game: Forbidden Word*

This is a fun game to play over the course of an evening. Begin by choosing a 'forbidden' word – it should be something that is said fairly often in this context, for example 'bar'. From this point onwards, whenever somebody needs to say this word, they have to replace it with the word 'gin'. So instead of saying 'I'm going to the bar', you would have to say, 'I'm going to the gin.' If you slip up and say the forbidden word, you have to take a drink – and then choose another forbidden word to add to the game. You can choose to replace it with a different word, or for real chaos, you can use 'gin' every time. As the game goes on, you can add more and more rules – like adding extra words to the start of people's names, or adding actions to certain words. The rules apply even when you're not talking to other players, so ordering a round of drinks can get pretty interesting.

## 23 SEPTEMBER

*Gineral Knowledge: Tonic*

Tonic water was initially intended to be only and exactly what its name suggests: a tonic, or medicine. Tonic's base ingredient, quinine, which is derived from the bark of the cinchona tree is a particularly effective anti-malarial remedy. Whilst it's highly probable that others had added gin to tonic water before, the story goes that the British soldiers in India, finding their daily 'tonic' water bitter and unpalatable, sought to soften the blow by adding gin, a bit of sugar and a bit of lemon juice. Funnily enough, it caught on and the gin and tonic was born.

## 24 SEPTEMBER

*Famous Birthday:*
*F. Scott Fitzgerald*
Fitzgerald was born on this day in 1896. Raise a toast to the man who mused 'First you take a drink, then the drink takes a drink, then the drink takes you.'

## 25 SEPTEMBER

With three months to go before Christmas, it's time to start thinking about getting your sloe gin underway. Go foraging for sloe berries, combine them in a jar with sugar and gin, and leave it somewhere dark for the magic to happen.

## 26 SEPTEMBER

On this day in 1969, The Beatles released their eleventh studio album Abbey Road, by Apple Records. Come Together and have an...

### Abbey Road

*2 measures gin*
*½ measure lemon juice*
*2 measures apple juice*
*8 mint leaves*
*soda water, to top*
*lemon and mint, to garnish*

Add all the ingredients, except the soda water, to your cocktail shaker, and shake vigorously. Strain into a highball glass full of cubed ice, top with soda and garnish with a lemon wedge and a sprig of mint.

## 27 September

If you head south from London's Abbey Road, take a quick left on George Street, a quick right on Seymour Street and head straight through Marble Arch, you'll end up on Park Lane. This information might come in handy one day. If it doesn't, we've simply directed you to the frothy, fruity and decadent Park Lane Special. You're welcome.

### Park Lane Special

*2 measures gin*
*½ measure apricot brandy*
*½ measure orange juice*
*2 dashes grenadine*
*1 egg white*
*lemon, to garnish*

Add all of the ingredients to your cocktail shaker and dry-shake for 10 seconds. Take the shaker apart, add ice, and shake again vigorously. Strain into a chilled coupette glass and garnish with a lemon twist.

## 28 September

*Gineral Knowledge: Jigger*

Cocktail craft is a very serious business but there's one word in the bartender's lingo that can give anyone not well-versed cause to giggle. That word is jigger. In case you're wondering if this is in fact a made up word, let us convince you it isn't. A jigger is a type of metal cup used for measuring cocktail ingredients. They come in various shapes and sizes, and will include numbers denoting measurements of liquid volume. Jiggers are essential for accurate and consistent measuring of ingredients, which will always make your drink taste better. According to cocktail historian David Wondrich, the name simply derives from the American term 'thingamajig'. Which is also a silly word.

## 29 SEPTEMBER

This Harry Johnson classic will put the pep in your step as the nights begin to draw in. It's a Martinez of sorts, with a brightening splash of Maraschino. Lovely.

### Turf Club Cocktail

*1½ measures gin*
*1½ measures sweet vermouth*
*¼ measure Maraschino*
*1 dash absinthe*
*1 dash orange bitters*
*cocktail cherry, to garnish*

Add all of the ingredients to a cocktail shaker or mixing glass, and fill with cubed ice. Stir for 30 seconds, and strain into a chilled martini glass. Garnish with a cocktail cherry.

## 30 SEPTEMBER

*Famous Birthday: Truman Capote*
US author Truman Capote was born on 30 September 1924. In his classic novel *Breakfast at Tiffany's*, the delightful Holly Golightly enjoys a cocktail she calls a White Angel: 'one-half vodka, one-half gin, no vermouth'. Why not mix one up and mark her creator's birthday?

# OCTOBER

## 1 OCTOBER

## Sake Day

Today is Sake Day, or *Nihonshu no hi* in Japanese. Sake Day marks the beginning of the sake-making season and is the most significant day in the sake calendar. Sake is a fermented rice drink which is brewed using a mixture of koji (a specific type of mould spore) and yeast. Sounds delicious doesn't it? No, it doesn't. But it is. It really is. If you aren't convinced, try a Sake Collins – a delicate, floral and refreshing gin and sake highball.

### Sake Collins

*1 measure gin*
*2 measures sake*
*½ measure lemon juice*
*¾ measure sugar syrup*
*½ measure grapefruit juice*
*soda water, to top*
*cucumber and grapefruit, to garnish*

Add all the ingredients except the soda water to your cocktail shaker. Shake vigorously, strain into a highball glass full of cubed ice and top with soda. Garnish with a slice of grapefruit and a cucumber ribbon.

## 2 OCTOBER

Today is the day after Sake Day and with any luck, you're a convert. Today, try a Sake Hi-ball. Crisp and citrussy; notes of gently fermented rice from the sake make for a surprising yet elegant gin highball. →

## Sake Hi-ball

*2 measures sake*
*1 measure gin*
*½ peach liqueur*
*1 dash orange bitters*
*soda water, to top*
*cucumber, to garnish*

Add all of the ingredients to a highball glass, stirring in cubed ice as you go. Garnish with slices of cucumber.

## 3 OCTOBER

Miso is a fermented paste that adds a salty umami flavour to many Japanese dishes. Like Sake, it uses Koji (the fungus *Aspergillus oryzae*), but with soybean and salt rather than rice.

These chicken skewers can be cooked in a griddle pan or on the barbecue.

## Miso & Gin Chicken Skewers

*Serves 4*

*625g (1¼lb) boneless, skinless chicken breast, cubed*
*8 spring onions, cut into 5cm (2in) lengths*
*2 red peppers, cored, deseeded and cut into chunks*

*For the marinade*
*3 tablespoons miso paste*
*2 tablespoons clear honey*
*3 tablespoons gin*
*1 garlic clove, crushed*

Mix all the marinade ingredients in a large bowl. Add the chicken cubes and marinate in the fridge for at least 30 minutes. →

Divide the marinated chicken cubes, spring onion and red peppers evenly among 8 metal skewers, threading the ingredients alternately. Brush with marinade. Heat a ridged griddle pan until hot. Arrange the chicken skewers on the pan and cook for 4 minutes on each side or until cooked through. Alternatively, cook under a preheated and very hot grill or on a barbecue.

## 4 OCTOBER

*Craft: Message in a Bottle*

Emails, texts and DMs might be a bit faster and more reliable (and, OK, you can actually control who you send them to), but there's something uniquely romantic about a message in a bottle. Next time you find yourself with an empty bottle, write down a note for a mystery stranger and send it out to sea.

## 5 OCTOBER

## World Teacher's Day

If there's a teacher in your life, whether a loved one, the educator of one of your children or even someone fondly remembered from your own school days, raise a toast to them – and perhaps even gift them a bottle of your favourite gin.

## 6 OCTOBER

Ready to feel old? *Meet the Parents* came out on 6 October 2000. Yeah – wow. Mark the anniversary by mixing up a Tom Collins, the favoured drink of the formidable Jack Byrnes, played by Robert de Niro.

First appearing in print in Jerry Thomas's *The Bartender's Guide* (1876), though most likely much older, the classic Tom Collins is so-named because the original recipe would have called for Old Tom Gin, a sweeter style than London Dry Gin. Timeless, refreshing and elegant. →

## Tom Collins

*2 measures gin*
*1 measure lemon juice*
*¾ measure sugar syrup*
*soda, to top*
*lemon and a cocktail cherry, to garnish*

Pour the gin, lemon, sugar syrup and a splash of soda water into a highball glass. Fill the glass with cubed ice and stir, top with soda and more ice, and garnish with a lemon wedge and a cocktail cherry.

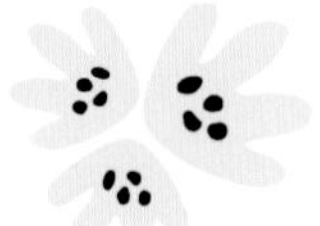

# 7 October

Autumn is well under way and that usually means wind and rain. Lots of wind and lots of rain. However, this is the sort of stormy weather we can all get behind. An aromatic and complex pre-dinner snifter, this is your excuse not to leave the house for at least four months.

## Stormy Weather

*1½ measures gin*
*¼ measure Mandarine Napoleon brandy*
*¼ measure dry vermouth*
*¼ measure sweet vermouth*
*orange, to garnish*

Add all of the ingredients to a cocktail shaker or mixing glass, and fill with cubed ice. Stir for 30 seconds, and strain into a chilled martini glass. Garnish with an orange twist.

# 8 OCTOBER

*Tip: Very Vanilla*

The subtle, sweet flavour of vanilla adds a lovely warming note to a G&T. Lightly bruise a vanilla pod and add it to a glass, then pour over a measure of gin. Leave it to infuse for a while (about half an hour if you can), then add ice and make your G&T as normal. Vanilla-tastic.

# 9 OCTOBER

On this day in 1701, Yale University was founded in New Haven, Connecticut, US. Known then as the Collegiate School, it was one of the nine Colonial Colleges chartered before the American Revolution. There are a number of Ivy League cocktails on a scale of tip-it-away to heavenly, and this is one of the best. The Yale Cocktail is a gin martini with the addition of a touch of Maraschino, which gives an astringent, fruited complexity. The recipe has evolved over the years with the original calling for Crème Yvette (no longer produced) which would have given the drink a slightly blueish hue as a nod to Yale's colours. If that's what you're after, you could experiment with tiny volumes of blue curaçao or crème de violette.

## Yale Cocktail

*2 measures gin*
*¾ measure dry vermouth*
*2 tbsp Maraschino*
*2 dashes orange bitters*
*lemon, to garnish*

Add all of the ingredients to a cocktail shaker or mixing glass, and fill with cubed ice. Stir for 30 seconds, and strain into a chilled martini glass. Garnish with a lemon twist.

# 10 OCTOBER

On this day in 1663, famous diarist Samuel Pepys wrote that, after having difficulty 'mak[ing] myself break wind and go freely to stool' he was advised to take 'juniper water' to ease his discomfort...yep, that's gin.

## 11 October

*Game: Blindfolded Bartender*

This is an entertaining way to liven up cocktail hour. Set up a tray of cocktail ingredients – different spirits, mixers, glasses and garnishes – and choose one person to be the blindfolded bartender. Put a blindfold on the chosen person, and then take a couple of minutes to move all the bottles around on the tray (just in case anyone was trying to memorize which bottles were where). The blindfolded person then has three minutes to mix a cocktail. They can ask questions about what they are holding, but it's up to the other guests whether or not they answer truthfully. You can decide whether the bartender has to drink their own concoction, or if tasting duties should fall to one of the other guests. You never know – you might invent your new favourite tipple.

## 12 October

### Pear Simple Syrup

Simple syrups are the home bartender's best friends. They bring sweetness to cocktails and the flavour combinations are endless. For an autumnal orchard flavour, try pear. The recipe below is for a simple syrup but you could experiment with spices and herbs such as star anise and cinnamon. Add a measure to a gin and tonic and garnish with rosemary.

*250ml (8fl oz) water*
*250ml (8fl oz) granulated sugar*
*225g (8oz) pear, chopped into chunks*

In a saucepan over medium heat, bring the water, sugar and pear chunks to a boil.

Once the liquid reaches a boil, immediately reduce the heat to a simmer and continue to simmer for about 10–15 minutes until the sauce thickens slightly. →

Strain out or separate the pear chunks. You don't need to mash the pear up through the strainer, just remove them from the syrup. Let the syrup cool to room temperature before using. Store in a sealed jar in the fridge for up to a week or store in the freezer for a couple of months.

## 13 OCTOBER

A super-speedy and delicious midweek supper.

### Pork with Gin & Caramel Pears

*Serves 4*

*2 William pears, cored and thickly sliced*
*2 tablespoons soft brown sugar*
*4 pork cutlets, about 250g (8oz) each*
*50g (2oz) unsalted butter*
*12 large sage leaves*
*2 tablespoons gin*
*250ml (8fl oz) hot chicken stock*
*salt and black pepper*

➜

Toss the pear slices with the sugar and set aside. Season the pork with salt and pepper.

Melt half the butter in a frying pan, add the sage leaves and cook over a high heat for about 3 minutes, or until crisp. Remove from the pan with a slotted spoon and set aside

Add the pork to the pan and cook over a medium heat for 3–4 minutes on each side, or until golden. Remove from the pan, cover loosely with foil and keep warm.

Melt the remaining butter in the pan, add the pear slices and cook for 2 minutes until golden. Remove from the pan with a slotted spoon and set aside.

Pour the gin into the pan and allow to bubble for 1 minute. Add the stock and simmer gently for 2–3 minutes, or until reduced and thickened slightly. Serve the pork and pears with the sauce, garnished with the crispy sage.

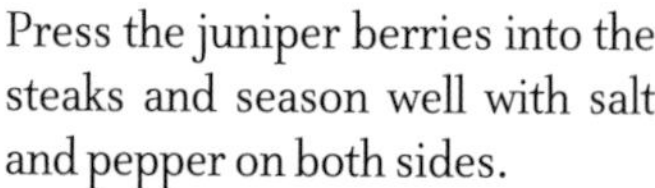

## 14 October

A wonderful, hearty combination of tender game meat and a rich sauce for a special occasion.

### Pan-fried Venison with Blackberry Sloe Gin Sauce

*Serves 2*

*2 venison steaks, about 150g (5oz) each*
*4 juniper berries, finely crushed*
*1 tablespoon olive oil*
*100ml (3½fl oz) sloe gin*
*250ml (8fl oz) hot beef or chicken stock*
*15g (½oz) butter*
*100g (3½oz) blackberries*
*salt and black pepper*

➔

Press the juniper berries into the steaks and season well with salt and pepper on both sides.

Heat the oil in a heavy-based frying pan and cook the steaks to your liking (2 minutes on each side for rare, 3 minutes each side for medium and 4 minutes for each side if you like them well done). Remove from the pan and keep warm.

Add the sloe gin to the pan and allow to bubble for 1 minute. Add the stock and cook for 3–4 minutes until reduced by half. Add the butter and the blackberries and cook for 3–4 minutes until the butter is melted and the berries are soft.

Pour the sauce over the steaks and serve.

## 15 October

*Famous Birthday: PG Wodehouse*

British author PG Wodehouse was born on this day in 1881. The creator of the iconic duo Jeeves and Wooster, gin pops up regularly in his works. A favourite quote comes from his 1958 novel

*Cocktail Time*, when the Earl of Ickenham asks his nephew, Pongo: 'What's the matter, my boy? [...] You look white and shaken, like a dry martini.'

## 16 OCTOBER

*Game: This is the Gin*

This is a gin-spin on a classic drinking game 'This is the Witch'. The players sit in a circle. The first player takes the bottle (of gin, of course), and holds it out to the person on their left, saying as they do so, 'This is the gin.' Instead of taking it, the second player must say: 'The juice?' The first player replies: 'The gin.' The second player now says: 'Ah! The gin,' and takes the bottle.

Now the second player holds the bottle out to the person on their left and says: 'This is the gin.' Now the third player must respond: 'The juice?'. Instead of replying, the second player turns back to the first player and repeats: 'The juice?'. The first player replies: 'The gin,' then the second player turns back to the third player and says: 'The gin,' at which point the third player can say: 'Ah! The gin,' and take the bottle. The game continues around the circle, becoming ever more complicated as more members join the chain. You mustn't touch the bottle until you have said 'Ah! The gin,' and you mustn't miss anyone out or stumble over your words. If you make a mistake, you must take a drink.

## 17 OCTOBER

*Gineral Knowledge: The London Beer Flood*

On this day in 1814, the London Beer Flood occurred. This fatal accident took place at a brewery in St Giles in West London, when a six-metre tall vat of fermenting porter burst, leading to hundreds of thousands of gallons of beer pouring out of the brewery and into the streets beyond. The St Giles area had previously been the inspiration for William Hogarth's print *Gin Lane*.

## 18 OCTOBER

*Tip: Ice is Nice*

We all know a good G&T should be served with ice, but some people worry about using too much in case they dilute their drink and end up with a watery cocktail. However, the best way to avoid dilution is actually to use more ice. The more ice you have in your drink, the colder the drink will be – meaning the ice will take longer to melt. So get those ice trays filled.

## 19 OCTOBER

## International Gin & Tonic Day

That's right, it's International Gin & Tonic Day! You know what to do.

## 20 OCTOBER

## National Pickled Onion Lover's Day (UK)

Today is National Pickled Onion Lovers' Day. Or it might be – there isn't much evidence to suggest it has been widely celebrated since 2012 – but put whatever plans you had for the day on hold and find some time to celebrate the pickled onion. There is a time and a place for everything and there is always a place for a cocktail onion in a martini. Honestly there is.

The Gibson is a classic gin martini, with an onion garnish rather than an olive or lemon twist – which gives a pleasingly unusual acidity. →

## Gibson Martini

*2½ measures gin*
*½ measures dry vermouth*
*cocktail onions, to garnish*

Add the gin and dry vermouth to a cocktail shaker or mixing glass, and fill with cubed ice. Stir for 30 seconds, and strain into a chilled martini glass. Garnish generously with cocktail onions.

## 21 OCTOBER

## Apple Day (UK)

It's Apple Day in the UK – the day to appreciate apples and orchards – and Sweden also celebrates the beginning of the apple harvest in events throughout September and October. Join the festivities and try a ginny twist on this modern classic. The perfect serve should be sharp, sour and ice cold.

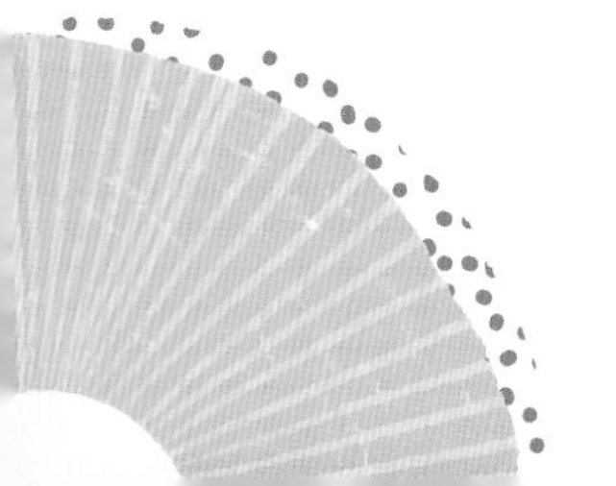

## Apple Martini

*1¾ measures gin*
*¾ measure apple schnapps*
*1 measure apple juice*
*½ measure lime juice*
*½ measure lemon juice*
*½ measure sugar syrup*
*pinch of cinnamon*
*apple, to garnish*

Add all of the ingredients to your cocktail shaker. Shake vigorously with cubed ice and double strain into a martini glass. Garnish with slices of apple.

## 22 OCTOBER

*Tip: An Apple a Day*
A crisp, juicy slice of apple makes a delightful garnish for a G&T. For extra flair, take three very finely cut apple slices and arrange them in a fan shape, then secure the end with a cocktail stick and balance it on the glass.

## 23 October

### Broadhurst Drive-by

*1½ measures gin*
*1 measure sweet vermouth*
*1 measure apple juice*
*1 dash lime juice*
*apple, to garnish*
*cocktail cherry, to garnish*

Add all of the ingredients to your cocktail shaker, shake vigorously and strain into a rocks glass full of cubed ice and top with soda. Garnish with a skewered apple fan and a cocktail cherry.

## 24 October

Missing summer? Well thanks to elderflower liqueur, you don't have to. Bring some sunshine into October with an Elderflower Mojito – the sharp sweetness of elderflower and the slightest bitter kick from a splash of tonic.

➜

### Elderflower Mojito

*1½ measures gin*
*1 measure elderflower liqueur*
*½ measure lemon juice*
*equal parts tonic and soda water, to top*
*cucumber and mint, to garnish*

Build all the ingredients in a highball full of crushed ice and churn. Top up with more crushed ice and tonic as needed and garnish with a cucumber slice and a sprig of mint.

## 25 October

*Craft: Gin Bottle Photo Frame*
This is an easy and quirky way to display your favourite photos. Take an empty gin bottle, clean it out and remove the label. Choose a photo and print it out. If you are using a gin bottle with coloured glass, like blue or green, this project will work best with a

black and white photo. If your bottle has clear glass, you can use whatever kind of photo you like. Carefully roll up the photo, taking care not to roll it too tightly – the key is to roll it up just enough to fit it through the neck of the bottle, but loosely enough that it will unfurl once it's inside. Push the photo into the bottle and, if you need to, use a pair of chopsticks to help you reposition it. When you're happy with how it looks, put the lid back on the bottle. And there you have it: a happy memory, caught in a bottle.

## 26 October

*Tip: Gin & Not Tonic*

If you are about to fix yourself a G&T and find that your tonic water supplies have run dry, never fear. Gin is nothing if not versatile, and happily pairs with a number of other mixers, including: ginger beer, bitter lemon, lime cordial, lemonade (especially pink lemonade), soda water and cranberry juice.

## 27 October

*Famous Birthday: Sylvia Plath*

American poet and author of *The Bell Jar* Sylvia Plath was born on 27 October 1932. She famously wrote volumes and volumes of detailed journals throughout her life. In one of her journal entries, she wrote about her longing for 'a magnificent stimulating home, where geniuses drink gin in the kitchen after a delectable dinner'.

## 28 October

Pumpkin season is upon us and it's time to do something with pumpkin flesh that doesn't involve pie, or putting it on the compost heap. Try this delicious, warming, ginny soup.

### Pumpkin, Orange & Gin Soup

*Serves 6*

*25g (1oz) butter*
*1 onion, roughly chopped*
*1 small pumpkin, about 1.5kg (3lb), peeled, deseeded and diced*

→

*zest and juice of 2 oranges*
*1 litre (1¾ pints) chicken or vegetable stock*
*3 star anise, plus extra to garnish*
*3 tablespoons gin*
*salt and black pepper*

Gently heat the butter in a large saucepan, add the onion and fry gently for 5 minutes until softened. Add the pumpkin and fry for 5 minutes, stirring.

Add the orange zest and juice, the stock and star anise. Season and bring to a boil. Cover and simmer for 30 minutes, stirring occasionally, until the pumpkin is soft. Scoop out the star anise and discard.

Allow the soup to cool slightly, then purée in batches in a blender or food processor until smooth. Pour back into the saucepan and reheat gently. Remove from the heat and stir in the gin. Ladle into bowls or mugs and garnish each with a star anise.

## 29 OCTOBER

With Halloween just days away, thoughts may understandably turn to apple bobbing, and what a cold, wet and joyless pastime it is. Make a stand this year and try a different sort of bob – a Fighting Bob. This punchy yet sophisticated highball is dry and herbaceous and keeps you far too busy to be outside in the cold chasing apples that other people have licked and bitten around a dustbin filled with water.

### Fighting Bob

*1 measure gin*
*½ measure Chartreuse*
*½ measure cherry brandy*
*¼ measure lemon juice*
*1 dash Angostura bitters*
*soda water, to taste*
*cocktail cherries, to garnish*

Add all of the ingredients to a highball glass filled with cubed ice, stir briefly and garnish with cocktail cherries.

## 30 OCTOBER

*Famous Birthday: Jerry Thomas*
Legendary American bartender Jeremiah 'Jerry' Thomas was born on this day in 1830. He is often considered 'the father of American mixology' and wrote *The Bartender's Guide: How to Mix All Kinds of Plain and Fancy Drinks*, which was first published in 1862. Why not celebrate his birthday with a 'fancy drink' of your own?

## 31 OCTOBER

## Halloween

Happy Halloween! According to its creator Harry Craddock: 'four of these taken in quick succession will unrevive the corpse again'. We beg to differ – anything with absinthe taken in quick succession is likely to leave you as a zombie so perhaps start with one and see how you go. Floral, aromatic and bracing flavours combine to make this a bartender's favourite the world over. →

### Corpse Reviver No. 2

*1 measure gin*
*1 measure lemon juice*
*1 measure Lillet Blanc*
*1 measure Cointreau*
*2 drops absinthe*
*lemon, to garnish*

Add all of the ingredients to your cocktail shaker. Shake vigorously with cubed ice and double strain into a chilled coupette glass. Garnish with a lemon twist.

NOVEMBER

## 1 NOVEMBER

# National Cinnamon Day (US)

Cinnamon brings a unique flavour to drinks – slightly spicy, slightly citrussy and sweet and woody all at the same time. Use cinnamon sticks as a garnish or make your own cinnamon and vanilla-infused gin.

### Cinnamon & Vanilla Gin

Simply put 1½ long cinnamon sticks, 5 or 6 crushed cardamom pods, ½ tsp vanilla extract in a sterilized jar along with 100g (4oz) sugar. Pour in 500ml (17fl oz) of gin, seal the lid, give the jar a shake and place it somewhere cool and dark for a week. Give the jar a shake every other day to help the sugar dissolve. After a week, strain the liquid through a muslin or very fine sieve, bottle it and drink it within 3 months.

## 2 NOVEMBER

On this day in 1973, Billy Joel's *Piano Man* came out, including the immortal lines: 'There's an old man sitting next to me / makin' love to his tonic and gin'.

## 3 NOVEMBER

*Famous Birthday: Dylan Moran*

Irish comedian, actor and poet Dylan Moran was born on 3 November 1971. Among his many comedic achievements is his stand-up show 'Monster', in which he observes: 'The most dangerous drink is gin. You have to be really, really careful with that...gin isn't really a drink, it's more of a mascara-thinner.' Well, it may be dangerous, but it's also delicious, so raise a glass to the birthday boy.

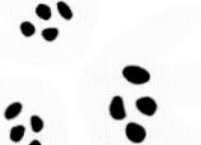

## 4 NOVEMBER

Less well-known than their spring-flowering relatives, the autumn-flowering camellias bring cheer in the dull days of autumn and early winter – much like this bittersweet and tangy gin sour.

### Pink Camellia

*1½ measures gin*
*½ measure apricot brandy*
*½ measure Campari*
*1 measure orange juice*
*½ measure lemon juice*

Add all of the ingredients to your cocktail shaker, shake vigorously and strain into a coupette glass. Garnish with a lemon twist.

## 5 NOVEMBER

## Bonfire Night (UK)

Remember, remember... Before heading out into the cold, make this delicious soup and serve in mugs with toast for dunking. →

### Fennel, Gin & Onion Soup with Gruyère Toasts

*Serves 4*

*75g (3oz) butter*
*1 head of fennel, thinly sliced*
*2 large onions, halved and thinly sliced*
*2 garlic cloves, roughly chopped*
*2 teaspoons chopped thyme*
*1 teaspoon dark soft brown sugar*
*3 tablespoons gin*
*750ml (1¼ pints) beef stock*
*1 teaspoon dark soy sauce*
*4 small slices of sourdough bread*
*100g (3½oz) finely grated Gruyère or Emmental cheese*
*salt and black pepper*

Melt the butter in a large saucepan over a medium–low heat and cook the fennel, onions, garlic, thyme and sugar for about 20 minutes, stirring occasionally, until soft and slightly caramelized. Pour in the gin and heat until evaporated. Add the stock and soy sauce and bring to a boil, then simmer gently for about 5 minutes. Season to taste.

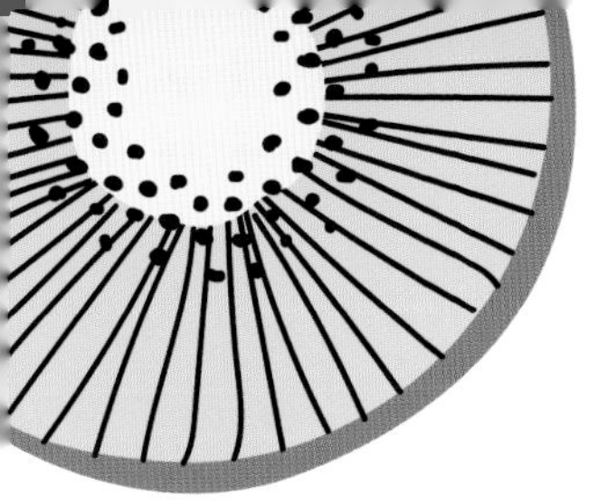



## 6 NOVEMBER

*Game: Pass the Hot Potato Parcel*
Everyone knows the worst bit about playing pass the parcel is that people try to hold on to the parcel in the hope that the music will stop while it's in their hands. To prevent this outrageous behaviour, add a little hint of danger to your next game. Wrap up a bottle of gin as the prize (of course), but in each layer that you wrap, include a piece of paper with a forfeit or dare. If the music stops while a player is holding the parcel, they have to unwrap it and complete the forfeit before the game continues. You'll be surprised how quickly the parcel makes its way around the room once people catch on.

## 7 NOVEMBER

*Famous Birthday: Albert Camus*
Albert Camus was a philosopher, author and journalist and winner of the Nobel Prize in Literature in 1957. We like to think he won on the merit of this line alone: 'Fortunately there is gin, the sole glimmer in this darkness. Do you feel the golden, copper-coloured light it kindles in you? I like walking through the city of an evening in the warmth of gin.'
*The Fall*

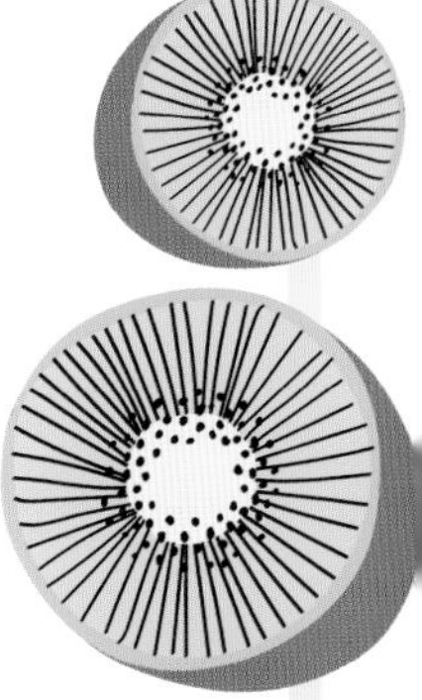

## 8 NOVEMBER

To kindle a golden, copper-coloured light in you, try a Golden Dawn. Hailing from 1930s London, this sharp and fruity snifter doesn't disappoint.

### Golden Dawn

*1 measure gin*
*1 measure calvados*
*1 measure apricot brandy*
*1½ measures orange juice*
*2 tsp grenadine*
*2 dashes Angostura bitters*
*lemon, to garnish*

Add all of the ingredients except the grenadine to your cocktail shaker, shake vigorously and strain into a coupette glass. Carefully add the grenadine to the finished cocktail, allowing it to float to the bottom of the glass to create a 'sunrise' effect. Garnish with a lemon twist.

## 9 NOVEMBER

*Craft: Gin Bottle Reed Diffuser*

Turn your empty gin bottle into a quirky reed diffuser to leave your home smelling lovely. Clean out the bottle and remove the label if you wish. To create your chosen scent, pour some carrier oil (such as almond oil or mineral oil) into a jug, then add your chosen fragrance oil (we suggest choosing something that mimics the botanical scents of gin, such as a blend of juniper berry oil and a citrus oil). You'll want about 15ml (1 tablespoon) fragrance oil for every 100ml (fl oz) carrier oil. Once you have a blend you're happy with, pour the scented oil into the gin bottle. Pop in some rattan diffuser reeds (you can buy them cheaply online), ensuring the ends of the reeds are immersed in the oil. After a few hours, turn the reeds over so the other ends are immersed in the oil. Soon the gorgeous fragrance will start to fill your room. Ta-dah! You can also make mini reed diffusers by using miniature gin bottles and trimming the reeds down to size.

## 10 NOVEMBER

*Gineral Knowledge: How Much?!*
You would be forgiven for assuming that the Brits are the world's biggest lovers of gin, but the country that consumes the most gin worldwide is actually the Philippines, getting through 22 million cases a year and making up 43 % of the world market.

## 11 NOVEMBER

The days are getting darker and murkier. Liven things up with a Fog Cutter.
Richly flavoured and wickedly strong, this complex rum punch is a Tiki classic. Its origins are as foggy as its name suggests but what is certain is that too many of them will have you on the floor. Quaff carefully. →

### Fog Cutter

*1 measure light rum*
*1 measure Cognac*
*½ measure gin*
*½ measure sherry*
*½ measure orgeat*
*¾ measure lemon juice*
*2 measures orange juice*
*orange, to garnish*

Add all of the ingredients to your cocktail shaker, shake and strain into an old fashioned glass filled with cubed ice. Garnish with an orange slice.

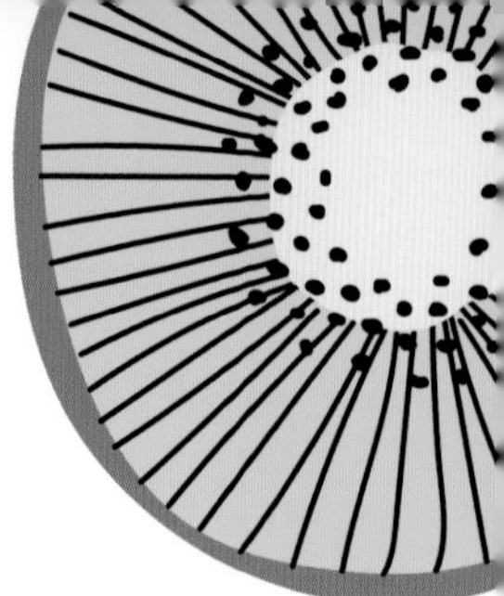

## 12 NOVEMBER

*Gineral Knowledge: Tiki*
The word 'Tiki' hails from the depths of Polynesian mythology, and was loosely and flamboyantly appropriated in North America in the 1930s. The term covers an entire aesthetic and liquid style, bright colours and tropical ingredients, Hawaiian shirts and cocktail umbrellas. Its founding fathers were two larger-than-life Californians; Donn 'Don the Beachcomber' Beach and Victor 'Trader Vic' Bergeron whose friendly and arguably contrived rivalry defined the era as much as the cocktails themselves.

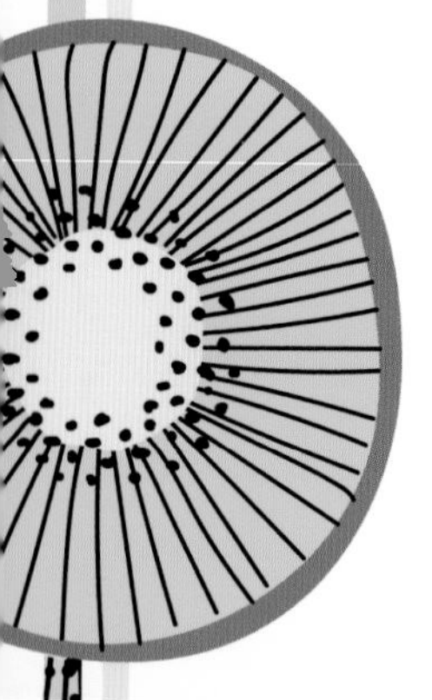

## 13 NOVEMBER

'Maids' are a group of sour-type cocktails shaken vigorously with fresh cucumber and mint. Light and refreshing, with crisp and clean flavours, this is the classic gin version.

### Maid

*2 measures gin*
*1 measure lime juice*
*¾ measure sugar syrup*
*3 cubes cucumber*
*8 mint leaves*
*cucumber and mint, to garnish*

Add all of the ingredients to your cocktail shaker, shake vigorously and double strain into an old fashioned glass filled with cubed ice. Garnish with sliced cucumber and a mint sprig.

## 14 NOVEMBER

Having been released in serial form throughout 1849 and 1850, *David Copperfield* by Charles Dickens was published in a single book format on this day in 1850. Celebrate with a glass of hot punch, as enjoyed by Mr Micawber in the novel: 'I never saw a man so thoroughly enjoy himself amid the fragrance of lemon-peel and sugar, the odour of burning spirit, and the steam of boiling water, as Mr Micawber did that afternoon.' (Some editions of the book say he is making this concoction out of rum, but of course we like to think the burning spirit in question here is gin.)

## 15 NOVEMBER

*Gineral Knowledge: Cocktails*
According to the list of 2020's bestselling cocktails compiled by Drinks International, ten of the thirty most popular cocktails in the world are made with gin – including the much-loved Negroni, which takes the number two spot.

## 16 NOVEMBER

The French Kiss (one would assume the creator was all out of creativity when it came to actually naming the drink) is a Negroni of sorts, with the wine notes of Dubonnet and the dry vermouth bringing a wonderful softness.

### French Kiss

*1 measure gin*
*1 measure Dubonnet*
*1 measure dry vermouth*
*lemon, to garnish*

Add all of the ingredients to a rocks glass filled with cubed ice. Stir briefly and garnish with a lemon twist.

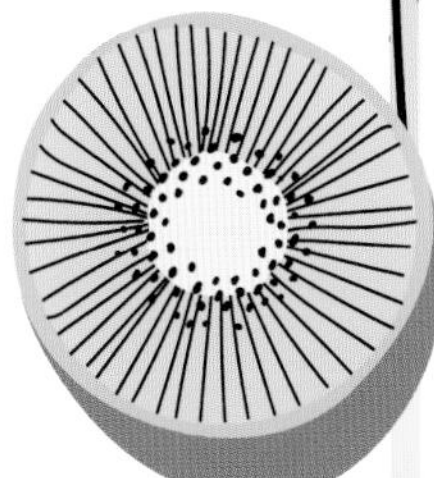

## 17 NOVEMBER

*Gineral Knowledge: Gin Palaces*
After the Gin Acts of the mid-1700s caused the price of gin to rise and consumption to fall, law changes in the Victorian era saw a resurgence in gin's popularity. Legislation brought in to try and prevent smuggling meant that the taxes on English spirits were made lower than those on imported ones. This saw the price of gin go down, and it once more became the drink of choice. Establishments known as 'gin palaces' popped up to satisfy demand, opulently decorated buildings with ornate mouldings, polished wooden bars and etched mirrors.

## 18 NOVEMBER

*Gineral Knowledge: 'It'*
In the early part of the 20th century, the drink of choice for young socialites was the Gin and It, a mixture of equal parts gin and sweet vermouth. This concoction is enjoyed by the characters of *Brideshead Revisited* after they ring the bell for pre-dinner cocktails.

## 19 NOVEMBER

Meaning simply 'gin and Italian vermouth'; though simple in its composition, this is a complex blend of botanical, woody and floral notes.

### Gin & It

*1½ measures gin*
*1½ measures Italian sweet vermouth*
*orange, to garnish*

Add all of the ingredients to a rocks glass filled with cubed ice, stir briefly and garnish with a slice of orange.

## 20 NOVEMBER

There's nothing to beat a hearty fruit crumble with lots of cream as the nights draw in.

# Pear, Apple & Gin Crumble

*Serves 4*

*750g (1½lb) pears, peeled, cored and sliced*
*500g (1lb) cooking apples, peeled, cored and sliced*
*2 tablespoons soft light brown sugar*
*1 teaspoon ground cinnamon*
*4 tablespoons gin*

*For the topping*
*200g (7oz) plain flour*
*100g (3½oz) butter, cubed*
*100g (3½oz) soft light brown sugar*
*25g (1oz) flaked almonds*
*25g (1oz) blanched hazelnuts, roughly chopped*
*crème fraîche or cream, to serve*

Put the pears and apples in a large saucepan with the sugar, cinnamon and gin. Cover and cook gently, stirring occasionally, for about 10 minutes or until the fruit is just tender. Transfer to an ovenproof dish.

To make the topping, place the flour and butter in a food processor and whizz well until the mixture resembles fine breadcrumbs.

Alternatively, you can place the flour in a large bowl, add the butter and run in with your fingertips until the mixture resembles fine breadcrumbs. Stir in the sugar and nuts, then sprinkle over the fruit and press down gently.

Place in a preheated oven, 200°C (400°F), Gas Mark 6 for 20–25 minutes until golden and bubbling. Serve with crème fraîche or cream.

## 21 NOVEMBER

*Gineral Knowledge: Gin Lane*

The well-known etching *Gin Lane* was created by 18th-century artist William Hogarth as a visual representation of the evils of gin. It was released in 1751, along with the accompanying *Beer Street*, whose happy and industrious residents extol the virtues of beer.

## 22 NOVEMBER

*Gineral Knowledge: Grenadine*
Contrary to popular opinion, grenadine – the non-alcoholic syrup – has nothing to do with The Grenadines in the Caribbean and everything to do with the French word 'grenade' which in turn has nothing to do with grenades and everything to do with 'pomegranate', which comes from the Latin 'seeded'. Traditionally made from the jewel-like seeds of the pomegranate, grenadine brings a tart sweeteness and a deep red colour to drinks. Try a Red Cloud – a gin sour, sweetened with apricot and grenadine and sharpened with bitters. ➔

# Red Cloud

*1½ measures gin*
*½ measure apricot liqueur*
*¾ measure lemon juice*
*1 tsp grenadine*
*2 dashes Angostura bitters*
*lemon, to garnish*

Add all of the ingredients to your cocktail shaker, shake and double strain into a chilled coupette glass. Garnish with a lemon twist.

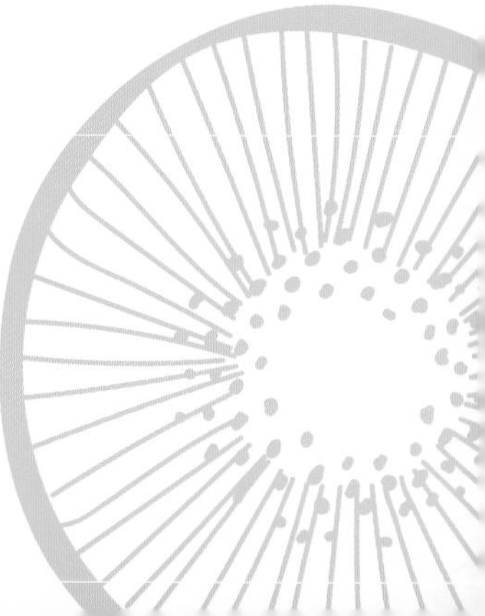

## 23 NOVEMBER

*Craft: Gin Bottle Candle Holders*

Next time you plan to dine by candlelight, gather together a couple of your prettiest empty bottles and turn them into candle holders. Clean them and remove the labels and buy some taper candles (sometimes sold as dinner candles) that are about the right size to fit snugly in the opening of the bottles. You may need to use a knife to carefully shave some of the wax off the end of the candles to help them fit. Then gently warm the wax at the bottom of the candle to help secure it in the bottle's neck. Voila!

## 24 NOVEMBER

## National Espresso Day (US)

Rise and shine with an Espresso Gin-Tini. A touch more aromatic than the vodka-based original, the key here is technique. For the desired foam, you must shake vigorously for a good 10 seconds, and ensure your coffee is of the best quality available.

### Espresso Gin-Tini

*1½ measures gin*
*1 measure coffee liqueur*
*1 measure fresh espresso coffee*
*½ measure sugar syrup*
*coffee beans, to garnish*

Add all of the ingredients to your cocktail shaker. Shake vigorously and double strain into a chilled martini glass. Garnish with the 3 coffee beans.

## 25 NOVEMBER

*Game: Who Nose?*

The classic drinking game Who Nose? is an oldie but a goodie. During the course of the evening, anybody in the group can place their finger on their nose. As soon as other members of the group notice, they must quickly and quietly do the same thing. The last person to notice has to drink.

## 26 NOVEMBER

On this day in 1946, *Casablanca* was released, giving us one of the most famous gin-related lines of all time: 'Of all the gin joints, in all the towns, in all the world, she walks into mine.'

## 27 NOVEMBER

Christmas is now less than a month away.
Pour yourself a stiff drink.

## 28 NOVEMBER

Round off a hearty winter meal with this lovely, lemony dessert.

### Gin & Lemon Posset

*Serves 4*

*300ml (½ pint) double cream*
*70g (3oz) caster sugar*
*juice and finely grated zest of 1 large lemon*
*3 tablespoons gin*
*raspberries, to top*
*shortbread biscuits, to serve*

Put the cream, sugar, lemon juice and zest in a saucepan over a medium heat. Whisk gently until the sugar has dissolved and bring to a boil. Take off the heat, add the gin and stir well. Pour into four glasses and chill until set.
Top each glass with a few fresh raspberries and serve with the shortbread biscuits.

## 29 NOVEMBER

Olive a little! If you've never tried your martini with an olive, today's the day. Adding an olive to your drink adds a salty, savoury tang that enhances the flavour of the gin and vermouth.

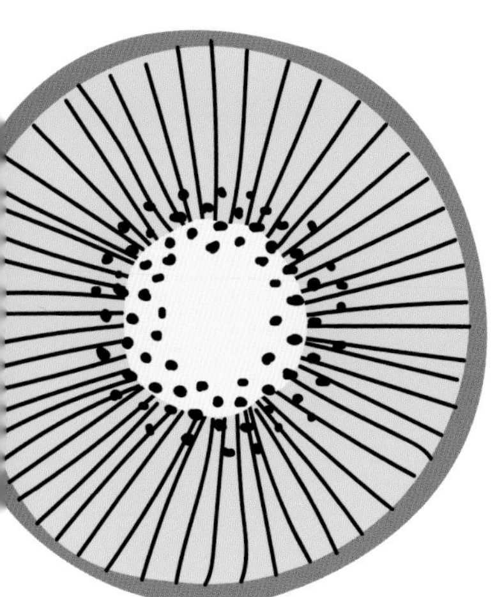

## 30 NOVEMBER

*Famous Birthday: Winston Churchill*

Now, take him or leave him, we're celebrating his martini here. A quirky and complicated man, Winston Churchill was known for his love of a tipple. When asked how he would like his gin martini prepared he replied 'I would like to observe the vermouth from across the room while I drink my martini.'

### Churchill Martini

*2 measures Plymouth gin*
*1 scoop of ice*
*cocktail olive to garnish*
*(1 bottle of vermouth, to observe)*

Add the gin to a mixing glass full of ice and stir. Whilst stirring, glance at the bottle of vermouth from across the room. Pour into a chilled martini glass. Garnish with a single cocktail olive.

# DECEMBER

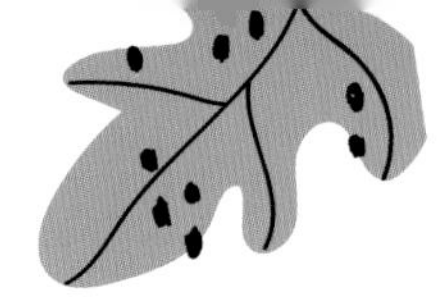

## 1 DECEMBER

'The gin and tonic has saved more Englishmen's lives and minds than all the doctors in the empire'.
*Winston Churchill*

## 2 DECEMBER

*Tip: Star Anise and Cinnamon*
To add a festive flavour to your G&T, try garnishing it with a pretty piece of star anise and a cinnamon stick. Their rich, spicy tones work beautifully with gin, and will make it even more warming.

## 3 DECEMBER

### Ginger & Cardamom Gin

For a warming, wintry kick to your gin, infuse it with ginger and cardamom. Enjoy sipping it neat, on the rocks, or long with tonic in a slightly spiced twist on a G&T.
Simply peel and chop 100g (3½oz) fresh root ginger and put it in a container with 6 green cardamom pods, cover it in 500ml (17fl oz) gin, put the lid on and let it infuse in a cool, dark place for 2 days (or 3 days for a more fiery taste). Then strain it and keep it in an airtight container for up to 3 months.

## 4 DECEMBER

### Bartender Appreciation Day (US)

If you're planning to head out for some drinks this evening, be sure to let whoever mixes your cocktails know just how much you appreciate their excellent work.

## 5 December

Prohibition ended on this day in 1933. Toast the anniversary in style with a Boxcar. Somewhere between the White Lady and the Southside – two classics of the pre-Prohibition and Prohibition eras, this is a perky and elegant gin sour.

### Boxcar

*1¾ measures gin*
*1 measure Cointreau*
*½ measure lime juice*
*½ measure sugar syrup*
*2 tsp grenadine*
*1 egg white*
*caster sugar, to garnish*

Dip the rim of a chilled coupette glass in a little lime juice and then in a small plate of caster sugar to create a sugar frosting around half of the glass. Then, add all of the ingredients to your cocktail shaker without ice and dry-shake for 10 seconds. Take the shaker apart, add ice, and shake again vigorously, and strain into the prepared coupette glass.

## 6 December

*Craft: Dried Citrus Slice Decorations*

The best use for citrus slices is, of course, a G&T, but they also make very beautiful decorations. Simply finely slice an orange or lemon and lay the slices out on a lined baking tray. Place them in a very low oven, 110°C (225°F), Gas Mark ¼ for about two hours until completely dry. Check after the first hour or so to see how they are getting on – some of the slices might dry out sooner than others. Leave to cool completely, then pierce the slices with a needle and thread them on ribbons ready to hang on your tree.

# 7 DECEMBER

## National Civil Aviation Day (US)

Today is as good a day as any to try an Aviation – a Harry Craddock classic created at the Savoy Hotel and first appearing in print in 1930. The Aviation is another of its creator's endless and innovative variations on the gin sour – elegantly balancing gin and lemon with bitter cherry and perfumed violet. Easy when you know how.

### Aviation

*1¾ measures gin*
*½ measure lemon juice*
*¼ measure Maraschino*
*¼ measure Crème de Violette*
*cocktail cherry, to garnish*

Add all of the ingredients to a cocktail shaker. Shake vigorously with cubed ice and double strain into a chilled coupette glass. Garnish with a cocktail cherry.

# 8 DECEMBER

*Game: Gin Pong*

If you feel like reliving your student days in a slightly more refined fashion, invite your friends to join you for a game of gin pong. Get into two teams and stand in your teams at either end of a table. Arrange some plastic cups in a triangle formation at either end of the table and fill each one with your preferred gin-based concoction. Teams take it in turns to try and throw a ping-pong ball across the table and into one of the opposing team's cups. If they succeed, a member of the opposing team has to drink the cup's contents (not including the ball!) and the cup is removed from the table. The first team to remove all the other team's cups wins.

## 9 December

*Craft: Gin Bottle Festive Decorations*

With Christmas just around the corner, here's an easy way to use your empty gin bottles for extra, ahem, Christmas spirit. Clean out your gin bottles and remove the labels if you wish. Go foraging for some festive foliage – sprigs of holly or other evergreens always work well – and arrange them using your bottle as a vase. If you have some pretty ribbon, try tying a cinnamon stick to the neck of the bottle for an extra fragrant touch.

## 10 December

So it's too early to stuff the turkey but it's not too early to start on the pickles.

### G&T Fridge Pickles

*5–7 small pickling cucumbers (or a normal cucumber will do)*
*1 tbsp juniper berries*
*170ml (6fl oz) gin*
*170ml (6fl oz) tonic water*
*juice of 1 lime*
*2 tbsp Rose's lime juice*

→

Wash and trim the stem tips from the cucumbers. Slice them in half lengthwise, and then in half again. Trim them to the length of your jar. You want the spears to fit into the jar and eventually be completely submerged in liquid when you are finished.

Mix the gin, tonic water, fresh lime juice and the Rose's.

Fit the pickle spears into a clean glass jar. Fill the jar but don't pack them in super tightly.

Lightly crush the juniper berries, and add them to the jar along with the liquid mixture. Top off with more tonic water if the spears aren't completely submerged.

Cap the jar tightly and refrigerate. Let the pickles 'pickle' for at least 2 days before eating. The pickles will keep for at least 6 weeks in the fridge.

## 11 DECEMBER

It might feel a bit too early to be thinking about Christmas yet, but now is a good time to start pulling together your shortlist of festive cocktails. For a wonderful, wintry celebration drink, try a Riviera Fizz – a sumptuous Champagne cocktail, bursting with hedgerow fruitiness.

### Riviera Fizz

*1½ measures sloe gin*
*½ measure lemon juice*
*½ measure sugar syrup*
*Champagne, to top up*
*lemon, to garnish*

Add all of the ingredients except the Champagne to your cocktail shaker, shake vigorously and strain into a chilled Champagne flute. Top with Champagne, and garnish with a lemon twist.

## 12 DECEMBER

If Champagne is a stretch too far, soda water makes for a wonderful fizz. The King's Fizz is a gin fizz spiked with orange bitters, which lift the flavours of the ingredients and give a fantastic citric intensity. The dry-shake is essential for achieving the desired light and fluffy texture.

### King's Fizz

*2 measures gin*
*1 measure lemon juice*
*¾ measure sugar syrup*
*½ measure of egg white*
*2 dashes orange bitters*
*soda water, to top.*

Add all the ingredients except the soda water to your cocktail shaker and vigorously dry-shake without ice for 10 seconds. Take the shaker apart, add cubed ice and shake vigorously. Strain into a chilled highball glass and top with soda water. No ice, no garnish.

## 13 DECEMBER

*Craft: Frozen Fruit Swizzle Sticks*
For a fun and tasty take on a swizzle stick, thread some of your favourite fruits – strawberries and raspberries work particularly well – on to skewers. Place these fruity kebabs on a tray and place in the freezer overnight, then pop them into your cocktails the next day. Swizzle stick and garnish, all in one.

## 14 DECEMBER

On this day in 1911, Roald Amundsen reached the North Pole. Pour yourself a North Pole in his honour. To all intents and purposes this is the Aviation cocktail turned into a milkshake, attributed to 'Trader' Vic Bergeron. →

### North Pole

*2 measures gin*
*¾ measure Maraschino*
*½ measure lemon juice*
*1 egg white*
*1 measure double cream, to garnish*

Add all the ingredients except the cream to your cocktail shaker, shake vigorously and strain into a chilled coupette. Garnish by gently floating the cream over the drink.

## 15 DECEMBER

*Breakfast at Tiffany's* was released in the UK on this day in 1961. Celebrate by crossing a sweet, aromatic martini in style. →

## Moon River

*1½ measures gin*
*½ measure apricot brandy*
*½ measure Cointreau*
*¼ measure Galliano*
*¼ measure lemon juice*
*cocktail cherry, to garnish*

Add all of the ingredients to a cocktail shaker or mixing glass, and fill with cubed ice. Stir for 30 seconds, and strain into a chilled martini glass. Garnish with a cocktail cherry.

# 16 DECEMBER

*Tip: Ice, Ice, Baby*
Take an ice cube tray and drop an edible flower, or perhaps your favourite kind of berry, into each mould. Fill the tray with water and leave to freeze. Next time you fancy a G&T, drop a couple of these pretty little cubes into your glass for a special flourish.

# 17 DECEMBER

*Famous Birthday: Noël Coward*
British playwright, actor and all-round wit Noël Coward was born on this day in 1899. Celebrate his birthday with a dry martini. He famously said: 'The perfect martini should be made by filling a glass with gin, then waving it in the general direction of Italy.'

# 18 DECEMBER

Why do we go to the trouble of mulling wine when we could be mulling gin?

## Mulled Gin

*150ml (5fl oz) apple juice*
*2 measures gin*
*1 cinnamon stick*
*2 star anise*
*4 whole cloves*
*1 dash lime juice*

Simply add all of the ingredients to a saucepan. Heat the liquid gently (don't let it boil) to steep the spices. After 10 minutes serve in a heatproof glass or mug.

## 19 DECEMBER

*Gineral Knowledge: Blind Pigs*

There's only one thing on our minds now: pigs in blankets. They're only days away but we understand that that might be too far away, so distract yourself with a fact about Blind Pigs. More often referred to as Speakeasies, Blind Pigs were illegal drinking dens where patrons had to speak quietly, or 'easy', for fear of being discovered. They rose to great prominence during the Prohibition era (1920–1933) in North America and have been celebrated and reflected in popular culture ever since. Dens of glamour and iniquity...those were the days.

## 20 DECEMBER

The only gift worth giving this Christmas is the gift of deliciously boozy homemade fudge. And it's okay if it's a gift to yourself. →

### Orange & Gin Chocolate Fudge

*Makes 800g (1lb 12oz)*

*500g (1lb) plain dark chocolate, chopped*
*400g (14oz) can sweetened condensed milk*
*finely grated zest of 1 orange*
*2 tablespoons citrus or orange gin*
*50g (2oz) white chocolate*

Line a shallow 18cm (7in) baking tin with nonstick baking paper.

Put the condensed milk and dark chocolate in a heatproof bowl over a pan of gently simmering water and stir until melted. Take off the heat, add the orange zest and gin and beat until the ingredients are thoroughly combined.

Pour the mixture into the baking tin, spreading into the corners. Level the surface and leave to cool. Chill in the refrigerator for at least 2 hours.

Lift the fudge out of the tin and carefully peel off the paper. Melt the white chocolate in a heatproof bowl over a pan of gently simmering water and then spoon into a paper piping bag. →

Snip off the tip and scribble lines of chocolate over the fudge. When the chocolate is set, cut into 2cm (¾in) squares. It will keep for up to 2 weeks in the refrigerator.

## 21 DECEMBER
## Winter Solstice

Happy Winter Solstice. Celebrate the shortest day of the year with a Kiss in the Dark – a satisfyingly strong and fruited gin martini with floral wine notes. Make sure you stir it for a full 30 seconds so the cherry brandy can open up and dilute sufficiently.

### Kiss in the Dark

*1½ measures gin*
*1 measure cherry brandy*
*1 measure dry vermouth*
*lemon, to garnish*

Add all of the ingredients to a cocktail shaker or mixing glass, and fill with cubed ice. Stir for 30 seconds, and strain into a chilled coupette glass. Garnish with a lemon twist.

## 22 DECEMBER

This traditional Christmas side dish can be made a day or two ahead and reheated.

### Braised Red Cabbage with Sloe Gin

*Serves 8*

*1 head red cabbage, about 1.5kg (3lb), finely shredded*
*50g (2oz) butter*
*2 onions, thinly sliced*
*4 tablespoons brown sugar*
*250g (8oz) tart dessert apples, peeled, cored and chopped*
*150ml (¼ pint) chicken stock*
*150ml (¼ pint) sloe gin*
*3 tablespoons red wine vinegar*
*1 teaspoon juniper berries, crushed*
*1 small raw beetroot, coarsely grated*
*salt and black pepper*

➔

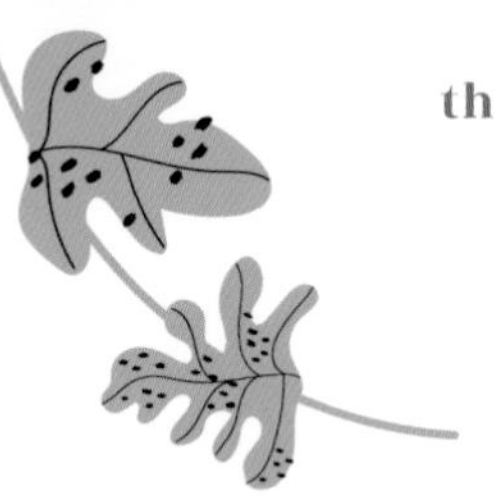

Put the cabbage in a large bowl. Cover with boiling water and set aside.

Melt the butter in a large heavy-based saucepan. Add the onions and fry, stirring frequently, over a moderate heat until soft and transparent. Stir in the sugar and continue to fry gently until the onions are caramelized and a rich golden colour. Take great care not to let the sugar burn.

Drain the cabbage thoroughly. Add it to the pan with the apples, stock, sloe gin, vinegar and juniper berries. Mix well and season generously with salt and pepper. Cover tightly and cook for 1½ hours, stirring occasionally.

Mix in the grated beetroot – this will transform the colour – and continue to cook, covered for 30 minutes longer, or until the cabbage is soft.

## 23 DECEMBER

Feeling festive? Gather your friends together for a rousing chorus of 'Gin-gle Bells':

*Gin-gle bells*
*Gin-gle bells*
*Don't we sound harmonic?*
*Oh what fun it is to drink*
*A lovely gin and tonic.*

## 24 DECEMBER

The sleigh bells will be ringing and gin-gling tonight so pour a Sloe-Ho-Ho for Santa – an ever-so Christmassy gin fizz for those of us who can't face any more mulled wine. If it's still there in the morning, it's yours. →

## Sloe-Ho-Ho

*2 measures sloe gin*
*1 measure lemon juice*
*½ measure sugar syrup*
*½ measure egg white*
*ice cubes*
*soda water, to top up*
*lemon, to decorate*

Add all the ingredients, except the soda water, to your cocktail shaker, and dry-shake for 10 seconds. Take the shaker apart, add ice, and shake again vigorously. Strain into a highball glass full of cubed ice, top with soda and garnish with a lemon twist.

# 25 DECEMBER

On this day in 1899, Humphrey Bogart was born. The Humphrey Bogart Estate teamed up with ROK drinks to create Bogart's Gin – a delicious, dry tribute to the great man himself. Bogart was a gin—Oh wait, it's Christmas! Happy Christmas and Happy Bogart's Birthday one and all.

# 26 DECEMBER

# Boxing Day (UK)

No Boxing Day walk is ever long enough to burn off Christmas Day , and sugar has now probably become part of your genetic make-up. Sleep it all off with a sharp, minty Knockout and start again tomorrow.

## Knockout Martini

*1¾ measures gin*
*1¾ measures dry vermouth*
*½ measure white crème de menthe*
*1 dash absinthe*
*lemon, to garnish*

Add all of the ingredients to a cocktail shaker or mixing glass, and fill with cubed ice. Stir for 30 seconds, and strain into a chilled martini glass. Garnish with a lemon twist.

## 27 December

*Game: Yum, Water!*
At this time of year we usually have all the family together, so it seems like a good time for a game (although this one is strictly adults only). You'll need a strong constitution (or a good poker face). Arrange a row of shot glasses on a table. Fill some with water, and others with clear spirits: vodka, sambuca, ouzo or, of course, gin. Muddle them all up until nobody knows what any of them contain. Then the players take it in turns to pick a glass and take a shot. After you have taken a shot, you have to smile at the other players and (convincingly) say: 'Yum, water!' If the other players don't believe you, they can challenge you. If you were lying and they catch you out, you have to do a forfeit. But if they accuse you of lying when it actually was water, the forfeit's on them. The sneakiest among you might even pretend to choke when it actually is water. Devilish...

## 28 December

It's now difficult to remember a time in your life when fresh fruit and vegetables were a thing. If you've forgotten to stock up on anything nutritious in your post-Christmas we-have-run-out-of-biscuits dash to the shops, there's a good chance that there are some berries clinging on to the remains of the trifle. Put them to good use in this wonderfully fruity gin mojito.

### Berry Collins

*2 measures gin*
*¾ measure lemon juice*
*½ measure sugar syrup*
*3 raspberries*
*3 blueberries*
*1 strawberry*
*soda water, to top*
*strawberry, to garnish*

Drop the fruit, lemon juice and sugar syrup into a highball glass, and muddle with a spoon. Add the remaining ingredients, fill the glass with crushed ice and churn. Top with more crushed ice and garnish with a strawberry.

## 29 December

It's okay if you don't know what day it is. Nobody knows what day it is. It's just that vague blob of days between Christmas and New Year's where you keep eating bits of cheese and finding cracker toys down the side of the sofa. And that's just fine.

## 30 December

If you need something bright and refreshing to cut through the bits of cheese that you've been living on for the last few days, try this refreshing, citrussy (read 'packed with vitamins') and not-too-boozy highball. →

### Sydney Fizz

*2 measures gin*
*1 measure lemon juice*
*1 measure orange juice*
*1 tsp grenadine*
*soda water, to top*
*orange, to garnish*

Add all of the ingredients to a highball glass filled with cubed ice, stir briefly and garnish with a wedge of orange.

## 31 December

## New Year's Eve

And so we reach the end of a glorious gin-filled year. Raise a glass to all the games you've played and cocktails you've made – and here's to the new year to come. Cheers!

# INDEX

## Food Recipes



## Gin-fusion Recipes



## Cocktail Recipes

# INDEX